KEEP IT 100%
BE TRUE TO YOUR "SELF"

BY

OCEAN SHAW

Foreword Written by Jerbrina Johnson, Esq.

ISBN 0-7414-5251-0

Published by:

INFIN∞ITY
PUBLISHING.COM

1094 New DeHaven Street, Suite 100
West Conshohocken, PA 19428-2713
Info@buybooksontheweb.com
www.buybooksontheweb.com
Toll-free (877) BUY BOOK
Local Phone (610) 941-9999
Fax (610) 941-9959

Printed in the United States of America

Published August 2009

DEDICATIONS

First, I want to dedicate this book to the Most High. Thank you, God, for opening my eyes to the realities of life and experience through my own trials and tribulations. Without You there is no knowledge or understanding-there is no TRUTH. Through this process, the truth and the acknowledgement of it has made me whole.

Second, I dedicate this book to my best friend, who is a true genius. I would like to thank him for inspiring me to follow my dreams and reminding me that anything is possible. I wouldn't have written this book without your constant prodding. Thank you, The ILL Genius, for believing in me.

Third, I dedicate this book to my little sister, Shari. I hope that you can use this information to make the best decisions for your life. Always remember your worth and value. Don't ever settle to be someone's second best. Always remember that you are the one and the only.

Lastly, I would like to dedicate this book to all of my readers. I sincerely hope that all of you find your best relationships and are the best persons you can be in them. Be true to yourself and everything else will fall into place.

TABLE OF CONTENTS

QUOTES FOR REFLECTION

"The tragedy of life is what dies inside a man while he lives."
-Albert Einstein

"A happy life is one which is in accordance with its own nature."
-Lucius Annaeus Seneca

"Small is the number of people who see with their eyes and think with their minds."
-Albert Einstein

"What we are today comes from our thoughts of yesterday, and our present thoughts build our life of tomorrow. Our life is the creation of our mind."
-Buddha

"Nurture your mind with great thoughts, for you will never go any higher than you think."
-Benjamin Disraeli

"To go beyond is as wrong as to fall short."
-Confucius

"Have no friends not equal to yourself."
-Confucius

"When we see men of a contrary character, we should turn inwards and examine ourselves."
-Confucius

"What the superior man seeks is in himself; what the small man seeks is in others."
-Confucius

"There is no happiness where there is no wisdom."
-Sophocles

"No one can be happy who has been thrust outside the pale of truth. And there are two ways that one can be removed from this realm: by lying or by being lied to."
-Lucius Annaeus Seneca

"If you would marry suitably, marry your equal."
-Ovid

FOREWORD

Jerbrina L. Johnson, Esq.
Atlanta, Georgia

"...And the truth shall set you free..." Though originating from *The Holy Bible*, this phrase has come to surpass ideals of religion to become a cliché often used when people are either seeking honesty or have been confronted with direct honesty. For those of you that continue to be engrossed by the strong desire to look deeper within yourselves for answers, your wish has been granted. ***Keep It 100%: Be True To Your "Self"*** is a raw, unforgiving guide for both women and men that find themselves asking "what the hell am I doing?" or "what now?" or "how did that happen?"

Love and relationships, along with the pain and confusion that come with them surpass gender, race, religion, and sexual preference. As a practicing family law attorney in Atlanta, Georgia, I have had the distinct opportunity to represent male and female, young and old, American, African and Middle Eastern clients. The issues, emotions and experiences, in essence, mirror each other. Though I've had the privilege of representing men and women equally, there is a distinct enhanced emotional plane that women often allow to overshadow clear, grounded thought. Whether it is because men are from Mars and women are from Venus...or because women have some unique hormone make up or extra-sensitive genes...the basis of it all is that women sometimes focus on anything they can in an effort to figure out why fate has yet to enter their lives, or why he won't commit, or why she's overcome with jealousy, insecurity or lack of focus.

We see movies and ask why we weren't born to live the life of Carrie Bradshaw, bathing in Christian Louboutin and Manolo Blahnik waters or the life of Oprah Winfrey, blessed with the gift of the tongue that has allowed her to become the wealthiest, most influential woman in the world. Men struggle with the moral obligations that come with marriage. What they have been taught is right goes against the inherent desire to partake in the beauty and uniqueness that is individualistic to every woman. They look at society and ask why they can't be in tune with their mate's emotions like Dr. Phil AND live the carefree baller/player/ladies' man life of a worldwide superstar like rapper, Ludacris? What makes these people so different than the rest of us?

The answer is simple and this book reaffirms that all we have to do is stop looking to others for confirmation, and instead focus on the image in the mirror. By appreciating our uniqueness, individuality and gifts, by embracing our past hurts and experiences, by re-opening our hearts and focusing on healing instead of revenge, we reconnect within and allow ourselves the freedom to be to thine own selves true.

Ocean and I have known each other for almost three years now. And ever since we met, she has always joked about how much self-esteem I have. I'll be the first to say I may never win a pageant if it is based on the smallest waist or the most well-toned arms, as those are not my strong points! She also jokes about the men I've dated and how consistently handsome they are. And I'll say this...I have always believed and continue to believe that just because 1, 2, or 5 people don't find me attractive, does NOT mean that I am unattractive. It just means they have a preference and I'm not it. I have never allowed rejection to determine my self-image and neither should you. I have never settled for a man that was not at my standard, because I believe he is getting the best when he gets me. So, I deserve no less.

Self-image and self-esteem are vital elements to success in any realm. Whether you desire to be wealthy or successful in relationships or famous, the key to being the best at what you do begins with an unapologetic sense of self. Coming from a small town in Mississippi taught me many lessons about self-worth. I grew up in a school district that had approximately 60% white, 40% black students but about 95% white and 5% black teachers. I participated in band, track, cheerleading, basketball, social organizations and was a gifted student. I also sang in my Baptist church choir and was president of an African-American empowerment group for teenage girls. I was placed in environments in which I was the only African-American, as well as environments where everyone was African-American. My family taught me to love everyone but not to trust people with a different skin color than mine. The mixed emotions and inconsistent advice drove me to question who I really was, how I really defined myself and what attitude was appropriate with one race versus another. I was tired of hearing from black friends that I sounded "white" and from white friends that I didn't really "act black." Luckily, the myriad of experiences required a deeper view into what I liked, what moved me and what I wanted to be. So instead of turning my back on my cultural identity or sheltering my intellect, I allowed it to make me the "me" I am today…comfortable in any setting regardless of race, gender or class. I was able to attend law school in a place where African-Americans have been traditionally ostracized and continue to be subject to racial epithets, and ignore the negative in search of my ultimate goal of becoming an attorney. Knowing I was penned to fail, I set my expectations above the average to be sure if I fell short, I would still reach the goal. And I did. This ideology is in direct correlation to the theme of *Keep It 100%: Be True To Your "Self."* Through positive self-esteem and strong will, which at times wasn't so strong, I satisfied one hurdle. The feeling of accomplishment has encouraged me to make new goals and set the bar even higher to see what can come when I believe in myself and stay the course. This book gives the reader a step-by-step guide to finding your inner strength and developing a stronger spirit that will guide you to focus on perfecting your talents. The message here is clear. First, make a DECISION to do better, be better and accomplish any feat you so desire. Next, have the DESIRE to succeed, even though you know you may fall. Finally, be DETERMINED. Even if you fall, determination will help you get up and get back in the race of life. As you read and assess yourself, these points and others serve to lay a strong foundation for achieving ultimate personal freedom through truth.

Fabulous. It's my favorite word, and I believe that if you don't think you are fabulous, no one else will. Often, people say they are, but they don't truly mean it. Just think about it. Can you say you're fabulous with tattered clothes and unkept hair as long as you're reading books to underprivileged children? Can you say you're fabulous with no shave and dirt under your nails if you're helping to feed the hungry two nights a week? Of course you can! It has nothing to do with money. It has to do with value. Do you value yourself enough to do a little something extra that makes you feel good about the person you see when you walk past a mirror? Do you help someone else feel better about themselves or help them solve a problem? Do you listen before you speak and take heed of the experiences of others? I have, and I truly believe that it is making me a better attorney and a better mate. Beauty, sexiness, swagger, that *umph*…all start within. Ever wondered how Jay-Z got Beyonce or why David Bowie and Iman have been married so long? To say opposites attract would be an understatement, but both of those men have an overwhelming confidence that has taken them from a less than humble beginning to immense success.

I encourage the readers to learn the basics. The common denominator among successful people is a strong sense of what they are good at (self-awareness) and a strong sense of who they are inside and out (positive self-esteem). Don't strive to be the celebrity, because their journey is unique. Use those tools to create the absolute best You.

Though my words are sweet as sugar, *Be True To Your "Self"* has refused to candy coat the *real*. The energy and spirit that unremorsefully come from the following pages are imperative to assist you, the reader, in overcoming the need to question why. It forces you to stop asking and start doing. Embrace the honesty of this guide, utilize the exercises for self-improvement, appreciate the story behind the gift of written expression and allow the questions raised to set your soul free…Peace & Blessings

Chapter One

OFFENSE

"We can easily forgive a child who is afraid of the dark; the real tragedy of life is when men are afraid of the light." -Plato

Since many of us are bombarded with "living and sharing" our world with others, we are often preoccupied with looking outward and pondering other's qualities. This concept can make looking inward a very neglected task. It seems as if the light is shining on others to see their uniqueness and character, but when forced to ponder on our own distinctiveness, the light seems to be very dim, if not gone completely. So, this book is written for people who desire to search within to discover who they are. In my opinion, the best way to begin discovering self is through one's thoughts, perceptions, and expectations. These three aspects are integral in shaping our behavior and explaining our reactions to our environment. How we think, what we think about, how we perceive other's behaviors, how we perceive situations, and what we expect from others and ourselves are all demonstrated in our behavior. Through our conduct is how others come to judge and define who we are as people, and these judgments can create identity. Once we as people are aware of how others see us and identify us, we have a choice. We can either adopt and accept the identity that is placed on us by others, or we can choose our own definition of SELF. The greatest part about identity is that we do not have to continue to adopt negative characteristics, and we can choose to enhance positive ones. Based on our decision of character, what we say and think about ourselves are manifested in our behavior and interactions with others.

In terms of making a choice about identity, who makes the final call-- the ultimate decision? The "decider" is the person I wish to reach with this book--the decider is YOU.

I have written this book from the standpoint of relationships. It is hard to sit down and evaluate our thoughts or reasons for acting a certain way. It is even more difficult to view our thoughts and actions when we are the victims in a situation. If we are accustomed to a particular behavior or thought pattern, it is hard to pin point the reasons for acting a certain way. It is when we are provoked by someone else's behavior that our thoughts are expressed through our actions. Relationships are one of the few mediums where we allow people to be close enough to us to activate emotions and thoughts ingrained in us by our past experiences. The way we connect or disconnect with others provides a "mirror" for observing and critiquing our inner self, and also provides a framework for identifying qualities that we perceive to be inhibiting or strengthening. The relationship advice provided by this book is geared toward a person who is single.

> **Side note**: Should you happen to already be involved in a "committed" relationship—and by committed I mean, already possessing a marriage license--use caution when reading this book. The concepts are intended toward those who have not taken that great step.

Not all the people who read this book will agree with or understand all of the concepts that are addressed. Some of you may even be offended by what you read. There can be a tendency in all of us to be fearful of looking too deep inside, and it is even more fearful to receive strong and negative criticism. However, without acknowledging and addressing our faults, we are unable to grow and become better as people. There are people in the world who shun the notion of truth and accountability. Yet, we do ourselves a disservice by living in a constant state of denial. Every now and then, we have to face the harsh truths in order to make our "dream worlds" become a reality. Sometimes in fixing a problem or devising a compromise to a dispute, it is important to get to the heart of a matter which may expose our most vial thoughts or nature. Everything cannot be solved by sweeping issues under the rug. Sometimes it is important to uncover those issues and deal with them in order to bring about healing. Religion is a great source of refreshment for our souls and overall well-being. Nevertheless, religion is a choice. There is still a person inside--You-- who makes the decisions. So, for the purposes of this book, religion and the practice of religion will be considered an identity and not a fundamental part of "you."

The reason that I went through those examples is to demonstrate why it is important for us to sometimes step out of our comfort zones and deal with issues that might be difficult and in ways that might be offensive. This book is written in a provocative way to lead you to be REAL with yourself. The concepts given here cater to people who want to take an HONEST look inside through the narrative of relationships and the role that they can play in them. I wrote this book for people who want to define their own identity, instead of solely adopting characteristics placed upon them by family, friends, or social networks. If one of your remarks is "My mother or my father never did that," or "None of my friends do that", then you don't have to abandon your beliefs, but I would like for you to also consider alternatives to these statements. I really must say that the intention of this book is for you to look inside of YOURSELF. If you reach the conclusion and your first remark is about someone else and what they need to do, you have missed the point. Now, don't get me wrong. I would love for you to share this with others, but if you go through the pages pointing fingers at others, you may still be blind to yourself. What many people don't realize is that before we interact with others, we first have to be WHOLE within ourselves. Becoming whole can keep us from questioning who we are on in the inside and prevent us from adopting negative qualities that are counter to our well-being. How can we expect someone to fill a void or provide answers to questions that we don't know **or** don't acknowledge exists? It is important to work on and examine ourselves first before we attempt to change or criticize someone else. Just as we have eyes to look outward, people have eyes to see us as well. When they observe us, what do they see?

In this book, I will be very direct, straightforward, and no-nonsense in my writing. I will address very sensitive and extremely emotional topics. There are also questions for self-reflection. Take the time to go back and really ponder the answers. Some people don't like to be told things, so it may sound like I am preaching. I am not preaching. I am only giving you some things to think about. The ultimate decision is yours in choosing what fits and what doesn't. Even if you respond with, "that is not me", you have identified yourself. If you feel you may be guilty of something that I bring up, accept it and find a way to be more positive in that area. If you don't like it, do something about it. You don't have to stay where you are and the power to change is within you. I fully expect that you will have an opinion once you reach the end of the book, but I would rather you have a better understanding and clearer vision of your "self".

Welcome to the ocean.......

Chapter Two

TRUE TO YOURSELF

"If you know the enemy and know yourself, you need not fear the result of a hundred battles. If you know yourself, but not the enemy, for every victory gained, you will also suffer a defeat. If you know neither the enemy nor yourself, you will succumb in every battle."

-Sun Tzu *The Art of War*

There is a song performed by Teddy Pendergrass that states, "You can't hide from yourself. Everywhere you go, there you are." This statement is very telling. No matter what happens or who you meet, you will always be true to yourself ([1]yourself being your "inner person") in the end. When we think of the word "true", the words faithful, loyal; real or genuine all come to mind. In other words, being "true to yourself" means that you will be faithful to the needs and requirements of your inner person. You can try to lie or change your appearance, but who you are fundamentally ("inside") never changes. The inner "person" that we attempt to bury or ignore for the benefit of others is always in search of freedom. So, instead of running from your inner "person", embrace it, because there is no way to separate from the "you" inside.

This chapter will discuss the concept of identity from two angles. The first discussion will be the importance of establishing your own identity before interacting with others.

---

[1] Definition of You-For the purposes of this book, "you" will refer to a level of consciousness. For example, there are foods that you like and foods that you don't. "You" will be the consciousness that knows that a food is liked or disliked.

Once we have a firm understanding and appreciation of self, we can then possess confidence and direction in dealing with others. The second discussion will explore the traits within that change little over time. If we are able to identify our core being, then we are able to identify our needs.

Establishing Your Own Identity: I Am...

Knowing yourself and accepting who you are on the inside are the most important keys and the first steps to getting into a healthy relationship with another person. These keys are important since one of the persons in the relationship will be you. So, who are you and what do you think about yourself? To know oneself is to be acquainted with, familiar with, and aware of the facts that make you unique. Oftentimes, we describe ourselves in terms of others' ideas of who we are and definitions provided by our environment. For example, someone could comment, "I am too fat." How do you know that you're fat? You are "fat" compared to what? We look out into the world and compare ourselves to what we see. Based on those images, we provide a definition for who and what we are, and then adopt that information as knowledge. The next step is to wait for others to confirm our "knowledge", so that we can convert it into identity. Based on this thought pattern, I would say that we know more about what people think about us, than know ourselves.

A positive outlook and firm understanding of self brings about confidence and courage. In order to go far in life, you have to believe in yourself and your capabilities. This normally starts with a positive self-perception and positive self-esteem. As implied by the words themselves, self-esteem comes from **you**, not someone else. We have to build our own praise first, and if we receive compliments from others, this should only *reaffirm* our thought. Conversely, if someone else does not share our opinion, then it should not tear us down completely. Instead it should be noted and skipped, because self-esteem is <u>the way we feel</u>

6

about ourselves, not the way others feel about us. Whether it is high or low depends on how acquainted you are with your attributes and how you personally label what is "good" or "bad" within you.

Knowing yourself involves being familiar with the characteristics and preferences that appear within you, and providing your own definition as to their meaning and significance, before you encounter others. This is important because other people are providing their **opinion** when they compliment or criticize you. Opinions do not necessarily mean fact. So why shape your identity based on others' opinions? Have you ever heard of the statement, beauty is in the eye of the beholder? That means that beauty is not a universal fact, although we can point to universal beauties. This is true for all aspects of personality. Some people will agree with your appearance, behavior and thoughts, and others will not. Are you going to change your identity based on every person you meet? This is why acceptance is the next important step.

If knowing is to be aware of your characteristics and qualities, then acceptance is to make a decision. This means that if you know how you are made up and you realize that this is who you are, then what are you going to conclude about this information? Some people conclude that their qualities are negative, which brings about insecurity and doubt. Insecurity can lead to a disapproving overall feeling of self. This is how plastic surgery has become a well-funded business, and how many people are misled about the personalities and security of their partners. What or who are we changing ourselves for? Why can't your characteristics be positive? Why aren't you beautiful? Why aren't you handsome? Because of someone's opinion? What about the opinion of the person that likes your appearance and attitude? Acceptance (of our unique makeup) is one of the most important tasks we can embark on. Decide to be happy with yourself. Decide to speak positively about your qualities. Decide to be pleased about who and what you are.

I am not saying that you cannot improve upon what you have, but it is important to have an overall healthy outlook or happiness with self by affirming your positive qualities, before embarking on change.

Remember, a positive outlook and firm understanding of self brings about confidence and courage. This normally starts with a positive self-perception. Find people who appreciate and value your uniqueness, and listen less to those who don't. Listen to constructive advice and not comments that are generated to tear you down. Some people will never cease to find fault.

Identifying Personality and Perspective

Since there are many aspects that converge to makeup a person, let's explore the concepts of knowledge of "self" and acceptance in a more tangible way. Everything about you is not wrapped up in your physical characteristics. Our bodies are more of an outward shell that house the real person inside. The "real" person is displayed more in our personalities and thoughts.

At this moment, I want you to forget about what is acceptable behavior. I want you to forget about notions of race and gender. Forget about social status and class, just for a moment. I want you to focus on aspects of yourself that are unique to you and you alone. In order to start thinking about who you are and what you want, ask yourself the following basic questions. Feel free to inquire more into your personality and preferences, than what I have listed here. The following are grouped according to category.

Personal Preference

- What kind of food do you like? Why?
- Is it because you are health conscious or could you care less?
- What kind of movies do you like?

- Do you even like movies or do you prefer to read books?
- What kind of music do you listen to?
- Do you listen to music all day and night or only at certain times?
- Are you a morning person or do you stay up late at night?
- Do you like to cook? Do you like to clean?
- Do you drive fast? Slow? Do you drive at all?

Comfortable Surroundings

- Do you like to stay home or do you like to go out?
- Are you a people person or do you like solitude?
- Are you family oriented?
- Do you want a large family atmosphere?
- Do you adopt friends as family members?
- Do you need to sleep in complete silence?
- Do you need time to yourself?
- Do you need people on top of you?

Sense of Responsibility

- Do you pay your bills and save?
- Do you spend every dime in your check and worry about bills later?
- Does work come before your family?
- Will you sacrifice so others can have?
- Does everyone have to work toward your happiness?
- Who is responsible for what, i.e. chores, child rearing, decision making?

- Who has the final say in a decision?
- Are you good at making decisions?
- Do you need time to make a decision?
- Do you need to hear all of the facts?
- Is it hard for you to apologize?
- Do you always provide excuses about why something didn't work out?
- Can you keep a secret? No matter what?
- Will you let others be punished for something that you did?

Personal Objectives

- Will you spare no expense in the pursuit of a dream?
- Would you rather work a job and receive a guaranteed income?
- Do you have a dream?
- What is it?
- Are you living it?
- Do you think your dream can be achieved?
- Did you give up your dream for someone else?
- Do you resent that?
- Do you think you are too old to pursue your passions?
- Do you think dreams are the luxuries of children?
- Would you hinder someone from chasing their dream?
- Are you a negative thinker?
- Will you step on others to get what you want?

[2]These are the types of questions that get you thinking about your personality, what you like to do and your perspective, and that help you get a better understanding of who you are. Continue to inquire more into your personality.

Discovering Fundamental Traits: Our Core Being

The above specific questions are good for determining our personal preferences. Our preferences and perceptions translate into our decisions and communication. They are also signals to our core beliefs and perspectives. Our core beliefs are more of a generalized quality that reflects our specific nature. Many independent decisions and thoughts can lead to a general picture of how you approach life. There are some aspects of our personality that remain constant and appear in some form in our everyday outlooks on life.

It is true that as we grow older, there are many things about us that change, but our fundamental qualities, base traits that make up our personality, do not change. Thus, it is important that we figure out what our fundamental qualities are, so that we may be aware of our consistent traits which may remain throughout the years. Since these qualities may continue, we should consider and contemplate them in determining our needs. If we can determine our needs, then we can make better choices in picking a partner.

In order to give you an idea of fundamental qualities, the following paragraphs will discuss two general traits. One trait will be a person who likes to operate within the standards set by society or their environment. Another trait will be a person who likes to set and create their own standard regardless of society. You do not necessarily have to be bound one way or another. In considering these two traits, I would like for you to ponder on the following

---

For further suggestions on personality, I suggest reading <u>Sextrology</u> by Starsky & Cox or some religious organizations have personality tests for finding spiritual gifts.[22]

questions as they relate to the examples and as they affect your own perceptions.

- How does a need to be "in tune with society" or "to create your own standard" translate to others in terms of communication?
- What effects do the above outlooks have on a person's needs or security when in a relationship with someone else?
- How does either trait come across to others in a person's mannerisms and actions?
- How do others come across to this person?
- How do these topics affect their view of the world?
- How do these traits affect how a person judges and sees others?

To make the questions more tangible, I will address these questions by use of examples of both types. Before I get started, I would like to say that there is no right or wrong outlook. The purpose in providing these examples is to help you gain a better understanding of yourself — how you think, and what you expect, so that you will make better decisions by identifying your needs. This will allow you to be true to yourself and act in accordance with your needs, when selecting a partner. Again, let me be clear, THERE IS NO GOOD OR BAD PERSONALITY TRAIT. **It is what it is.** This is not the time to be judgmental and shun a way of thinking because you don't agree. This is the time to determine what thoughts resonate with you (which qualities represent you) and embrace (identify and accept) those qualities whatever they may be.

Side note: There are positive and negative aspects to your qualities. The point of acknowledgement and acceptance is to help you identify your verbal and nonverbal communications, along with your perceptions. Knowing this information about yourself will help you to interact with

---

others, especially in romantic relationships. Many people say that opposites attract in dating. This can be true, but only to a certain extent. A relationship is two people coming together and working towards the "same goals" in life. A relationship is a union. If your perspective on life and how it should be lived is different from your partner's, how can you come together as a cohesive unit? For example, you want to discipline children through time out, and your partner wants to use physical contact. When the time for discipline arises, you may find yourself undermining your partner. Discovering your perspective and aligning yourself with it is important in laying the foundations of your relationship. The foundations of your relationship start with you, the individual, and your partner, the individual. By coming together, you both create the foundation of your relationship.

The following examples will provide an outlook of perspectives and how they manifest themselves in a relationship.

Do You Color Within the Lines?: Adhere to Social Norms

If your personality type cares what others think about you, then you may have a tendency to be very "political" in your behavior. You may try not to offend anyone, making sure that you use politically correct language. You may subscribe to social delineations of gender and race. In other words, women may have a specific role to play and so do men. A certain behavior may be expected from people in your social or financial class or famous stature. Whatever societal attributes you associate with will most likely be represented in its fullest form. Social status and adherences to status and class may be very important for your social circle. Therefore, your friends and close associates might also reflect who you would like to portray yourself to be.

So, what kind of needs does this personality have? What kind of partner would be able to fulfill the needs of a person exhibiting this trait? This person may most likely need a partner that cares about their social appearance as well. This partner may probably need to be educated or successful in business or their area of profit. They would have to be able to communicate effectively with others without embarrassment to you or themselves, and a number of personal accomplishments won't hurt. This person would have to embody what is acceptable of a person in that stature through behavior and speech. The persons responsible for setting the bar of approval will have to validate your partner as being an acceptable choice. Personal maintenance may be very important in all aspects of life. A "fall from grace" could test the limits of this relationship.

Are You the Norm?: Create Your Own Standard

If your personality trait is the antithesis or the opposite of the above example, then you may be laid back and free spirited. Instead of trying to please society, you may be more involved in what you find interesting, whether it is socially acceptable or not. You set your own pace and your own standard. You may not have strict ideas of gender roles and are willing to see what fits you. Your personality may be the type to say what you feel or what you think regardless of social backlash. Your BEST fit may be with someone who is also free spirited, but it will be important for you to figure out what you like and how far you are willing to go. You may book a spontaneous vacation to Jamaica with someone you just met three weeks ago, but not be willing to participate in hedonism. Free spiritedness does not always express itself in the same ways. You may need to find out where you are on that spectrum.

Possible Repercussions

I hear some of you saying, that you don't agree. Let's look at what happens when you choose the opposite. If you care what society thinks about you, and you decide to partner with someone who could care less, then every time the two of you are in a social setting, you could feel that your partner is embarrassing you. Why? Because your partner is an extension of you, a representative of YOU. Then, in

14

order to save face, you may try to reign in your partner, which will stifle their freedom to be who they are. Your partner may soon start to rebel and "embarrass" you "intentionally". After some time, you and your partner may make less social appearances together, or you may even forgo activities that you would like to participate in, because they require your significant other to be present. The kind of statement that makes in your relationship is that you are ashamed of your partner or you do not accept them for who they are. This can bring about negative feelings on both sides. In the eyes of your partner, it may seem that you think you are "better than" and "above" them. Once your partner's self esteem is gone or their interpretation of how you see them has been destroyed, so is your relationship.

Vice versa, you are a free spirit and your partner seems like a prude. You are continually frustrated by their need to be accepted by people you could care less about. You feel bound, because they are bound. All you want to do is run away. So, now you may not be spending time with your partner. Instead, you would rather spend time with other people that allow you to be yourself. Your partner may now begin to feel neglected and as if you are no longer interested. There seems to be a gaping hole in your relationship and a growing distance between you. This phenomenon exists because to "be with you" is to have your physical presence and attention. When that is gone, you have left the relationship. Whether you have actually left the relationship is of no importance. It is only a matter of time before the physical catches up with the mental and emotional.

The point of these examples is to demonstrate why it is important to BE YOURSELF, whatever that is. Also, it is important to acknowledge how you perceive the world and what affect your perceptions have on your needs. This is so that you can make decisions to positively affect your life and relationships. The previous examples show us what can happen in relationships when we are not aware of how we think or what we expect, and how not being true to ourselves can bring about not only our negative emotions, but negative thoughts and feelings in others. There are many aspects to our personality, so the more that we learn about ourselves, then the more we can be faithful to our needs. Embrace (love) who you are and accept it, because it manifests itself anyway, and there is nothing you can do to stop it. Why? Because you are who you are, and you cannot run from or deny yourself. No matter what we attempt in life or what we accomplish, we will ALWAYS be true to ourselves in the end. There is no right or wrong when it comes to our base traits, only THERE IS.

True to Yourself is to act in accordance with your needs.

Chapter Three

LUGGAGE OR WRIST BAG-WALLET?

"If you are moving forward and looking backward, then your past is probably ruining your relationships."   -Ocean Shaw

The second key to determining who you are is figuring out where you came from. What kind of impact did your past have on your personality, expectations, general outlook, desires and most importantly your needs? All of us have been shaped in some way by our upbringing and interactions with others. Every time you involve yourself with a person, you are creating a new experience that stays with you in some way, shape or form. Every encounter is not necessarily memorable, but does play a role in the bigger outlook that has been derived from that experience and other experiences similar to it. Think about your first encounter with a teacher. Not all teachers are memorable, but an outlook of teachers in general has been formed throughout the years. Some teachers are more noteworthy than others; some teachers were mean; and others showed that they cared about your well-being. Some subjects were boring and others fascinating. All of these experiences make up your outlook on education. The same can be said of relationships.

Encounters and experiences with your parents, friends, partners, family members, coworkers, or random people in the street can impact your outlook on relationships. Some of those encounters were more noteworthy than others; some were mean; some showed that they cared about your well-being; others were boring and some were fascinating.

This is only partially important. What is most important is the kind of effect that it had on YOU. Did it create luggage? Or were you able to walk away with a wallet or a wrist bag? Have you turned your luggage into a carrying case? Or are you still collecting more pieces? **Ultimately, what kind of baggage are you carrying around?**

Discovering Issues: What Are You Carrying?

There are all kinds of baggage with all kinds of designs. Designs entail how the issues manifest themselves. Here is the tough part. The first step is acknowledgment. "Yes, Ocean. I have baggage." Guess what? So does everyone else, whether they acknowledge it or not. The second step is realization. What kind of design does your baggage have?

The following are questions to give you an idea of how your past can influence your present.

- Are you ignoring your past, and therefore suppressing it?
- Do you throw tantrums?
- Do you replicate your experience on others?
- Do you talk about it incessantly?
- Do you blame others for everything?
- Is nothing your fault?
- Are you a runner?
- Do you have psychotic episodes?
- Are you destructive?
- Are you self-destructive?
- Do you overcompensate for what you lack?
- Are you controlling?

How is the design imprinted on your life?

I am about to address some issues that some of us are dealing with.

What kind of issues do you have?

- Do you have "Daddy" issues? "Mommy" issues?
- Do you have abandonment issues?
- Do you think that you are inadequate – physically, intellectually, emotionally?
- Are you afraid of failure?
- Do you drink to escape from your problems?
- Do you use drugs to self-medicate?
- Do you have reckless tendencies i.e. need for speed, provoke people to hurt you?
- Were you sexually assaulted as a child? By a family member?
- Did you sexually assault someone?
- Were you raped?
- Were you beaten as a child?
- Were you beaten in your relationships?

- Are you beating your partner?
- Were you neglected as a child?
- Did your parents give you up for adoption?
- Are you jealous of your siblings?
- Are you in competition with your family members?
- Were you told that your sibling was better than you?
- Were you spoiled as a child?
- Did people tell you that you were better than everyone else because of your looks, your race, your gender, or your social status?
- Did your parents love your sibling(s) more than you?
- Were you ignored?
- Will you do anything for attention?
- Are you divorced?
- Are you a product of a divorced home?
- Do you want your parents to get back together?
- Are you determined to make their new spouse miserable?
- Did they tell you that you would never amount to anything?
- Did they tell you that you were ugly? Too skinny? Too fat? Not light enough? Too dark?
- Did they tell you that no one would ever love you?

What kind of negativity was placed on or ingrained in you from your past?

Now, what kind of impact did that have on you? What did those experiences cause you to need TODAY?

Parenting Issues

- Are you really looking for your father instead of a husband?

- Is a lack of a father causing you to be a failure as a father to your children because you are still sulking and playing the victim?

- Does the lack of a father or mother cause you to not want children yourself?

- Are you compensating for lack of a parent by being the best parent you can be to your children?

- Have your experiences caused you to hate the same gender children as yourself? The opposite gender?

Expression of Love and Affection

- Does your partner have to constantly reassure you of their love for you and that they don't want anyone else?

- Do you require constant compliments and attention?

- Does someone have to remind you what you are worth?

- Does your faith have to be restored in others?

- Does your partner have to be patient with sex until you are comfortable?

- Do they have to take it slow and remind you that it is them and not your attacker?

- Do you not like sex period?

- Do you equate sex with love and affection? Abuse?

- Do you abuse your own body because others have constantly abused you?

- Does your partner have to refrain from yelling and using abusive language?

Dependency

- Are you holding on to a relationship that you know is over?

- Are you scared to let go because you won't find anyone else?

- Are you holding on so your partner can't be with someone else?

All of these requirements and responses to issues from your past play a major role in who you have become and what you need in order to maintain a healthy relationship.

The Disclosure of Issues

Some of you don't want to discuss these issues because you can't handle it, and it is hard to handle. Others don't want to discuss these issues because they don't want to know or they are afraid. If you are suffering with these issues, you have a responsibility to yourself and your partner to deal with what is affecting you. Also, the ability to choose a suitable understanding partner will require that you are a good judge of character, able to read nonverbal communication, and that you have tough skin should you choose poorly. This is going to make the difference in what kind of partner you will have and whether your needs are met.

What I am about to say is for the time that you are considering a life-long partner. I will repeat, "The following statements are for when you are considering a life-long partner." Your partner should be aware of the issues you are dealing with. I hear what you are saying, "They are going to run away from me, if I tell them about my past." If they are going to run, they are going to run anyway. It is better to get a person who is not understanding and not ready to deal with your issues out of the way, so your BEST partner can come along, rather than wasting time with someone that loves you CONDITIONALLY. I only want to be with you if..........

That person, a conditional partner, doesn't love you for all that made you who you are. They love a misrepresentation of you, because if they found out everything about you, they would not have the same feelings. Why lie to yourself and your partner, and why have them lie to you? You aren't who they want, and they aren't who you NEED. So, set them free, so you can be free yourself. It is very unhealthy to be with a person that makes you feel terrible for what has happened to you or for bad decisions you've made. It is also unhealthy to be with a person who does not and cannot understand how your experiences and decisions have come to affect you. It doesn't mean that you have to celebrate the negative occurrences of your life, but these occurrences do have to be acknowledged and accepted in order to begin forward movement in a healthy manner. At the very least, your partner should desire to be familiar with all of the things that can affect you.

Most of you are not going to disclose this kind of information to your partner for the following reasons: 1) you don't trust them; 2) you are pretending to be someone you are not; 3) you haven't dealt with the issue, or 4) your past is threatening to unravel you. So, with that I ask, "How do you expect to get what you need when you aren't being honest with yourself or your partner?" If you love that person and they love you, there shouldn't be anything the two of you can't handle. If your partner LOVES you, they won't be quick to run as soon as they hear that kind of information. It should draw them closer to you because of the disclosure, and they should be equipped to handle this issue either through personal experience or past situations that provide empathy and understanding. Your BEST partner should have life experiences that help them either comprehend and appreciate, or identify with you at the very least. In this way, there is a common understanding of your plight, and all aspects of dealing with your issue are communicated verbally and nonverbally.

Reading Your Partner

Sometimes in our reactions to news, our words do not line up with our physical expressions. So, it is important that we are aware of both in ourselves and in others. Remember, you have the benefit of knowing your secrets before your partner does. When evaluating a partner, bring up general topics that are related to your issue, and then pay attention to their verbal and nonverbal response. For example, ladies, you do not have a relationship with your father. In your mind, you want to date a man that has "fatherly qualities" i.e. loves children and wants to have a family. Before you decide to have sex, especially unprotected sex, with a potential partner, why not broach the idea of children? Look to see if he squirms, or avoids the topic or talks about children so far in the future, that you know you won't be present when that time comes. If you receive a negative or apprehensive response from him at the mere mention of children, then imagine his response if you told him that you were pregnant. There are cues in our demeanor and actions that signal towards our actual feelings and thoughts. Nonverbal communication is just as important and as worthy of our attention as verbal communication. In the alternative, you can tell someone something and their response is completely nonverbal, but communicates the intention, such as a hug or a kiss. There are many signs and signals that are given in communication. Our ability to recognize those signs will allow us to choose better mates who are able to fulfill our needs and handle our issues.

The Timing of Discloure: When to Tell and Why

I know you may still have questions about timing. I cannot really answer that because people are in different stages of their relationships. I stated that you should consider telling a life-long partner. This is someone who has demonstrated an interest in being indefinitely committed to you, i.e. marriage. It will be important for you to determine the intentions of your partner. This means that you put your desires on hold and listen to what your partner is saying. Have a conversation with them about where they think the relationship is going or about their desires for the future. Are you in them? Are they with you to pass the time? Do they make comments as if they don't know what they want to do? If that is the case, then your relationship may not be going anywhere, and all you are doing is wasting time. That may not be the person to tell your dark secrets to.

In the end, timing is very important. Some people wait too late, and some people tell things too early. Normally, your gut will tell you when to divulge information. What usually happens is your partner will make a comment that will trigger information that you have been holding. Then comes a sense of panic, and stress takes over your body. After that, there is a burning feeling to tell the truth. You are not really listening to what your partner is saying, instead you are trying to decide if you should say something or not. If you are experiencing these symptoms, then that may be the time to say something. If you decide not to share your imperfections, then the next opportunity may be too late.

Side note: This advice is equally true for your more recent past. If there is anyone else who is familiar with your distant or recent past, there is always the possibility of exposure. If you are the one to share the information, then you can control how it is presented. It is always better that your partner hears news from you than someone else. When it comes from someone else, you have to combat 1) embarrassment from being surprised, 2) lack of trust from not saying it yourself, 3) the possibility of misinformation from people who heard it secondhand, and 4) the pain of the news itself. Adopt the perspective of politicians, once its out, it's out, they can never bring you down with that information again.

Some of us start the relationship telling all of our issues upfront and run the person away before they get the opportunity to learn about us. In this case, you have become your issues instead of your issues becoming obstacles that YOU have overcome. This is an example of moving forward and looking backward. Your past does not have to define you. **Your past can be the catalyst that built character, maturity, and appreciation in you.** The timing will be based on how well you are able to judge the situation and listen to the comments made by your partner.

Chapter Four

PREVIOUS CATS

"We must be responsible enough to admit that the person we are involved with is only a reflection of our present state of development." -Alvin Morrow *Breaking the Curse of Willie Lynch*

Most of us are at the point where we have some form of baggage from previous relationships. Hardly anyone walks away from an interaction with another person without being affected in some way. Some effects lasting a lifetime. There is nothing wrong with being affected by a situation or encounter, but what is important is how you allow yourself to deal with the experience. We will take a look at some examples of how we normally deal with experiences and allow them to become baggage.

A relationship has turned for the worse, and now you are holding negative feelings not only for that person, but all members of that gender. With that attitude, comments of the following arise: "I hate men." and "All bitches are crazy." This attitude leads to a declaration of "I refuse to have feelings like this for someone ever again," or "I'm just going to be a player." The real resolve that you should normally start with is that you hate that particular man, or that particular woman is crazy. To take an experience with one person and attribute that characteristic to a general population is counterintuitive and erroneous. Okay, for the naysayer, if your statement is correct i.e. "I hate men", then what is your alternative, women? Deep down inside you want a relationship with a man (for the men, a woman). The key is that you don't want a relationship with a particular type of man or woman. When a relationship has ended badly or with extreme feelings of pain, this is a real important time to conduct an internal evaluation.

The first question is what type of partner do you want? For more help with this aspect keep reading and re-read the previous chapters if necessary. The second question is what type of partner was your previous partner? What was it about them that was so wrong? Some of you have a pattern of the same type of partner with the same negative traits, and that characteristic definitely needs to be identified and addressed. What is it about these traits that attract you? Why do you lean towards that type of partner, when it seems to be counter to your productivity and happiness? The answer could be that you like an aspect of a trait but not want that trait in abundance. For example, some women may say that they want a "thug". Actually, that is not the truth. What those women really want is a man with a backbone; a man that knows how to handle himself in negative situations; a man that commands respect in his persona. What all of these attributes lead up to is SECURITY. Another example is some men may express a desire towards a "ghetto woman" or a "stripper". Actually, for some men, that is not entirely the case. What these men really want is a woman that is comfortable with her body and her sexuality; a woman that is open minded sexually; a woman that likes to take care of herself physically or a woman that is able to speak her mind and articulate exactly what she wants.

Identifying The Past in Your Present

If the traits have not been identified, then you run the risk of bringing your past into your present. So, to revisit the prior complaint and get the whole picture of the mental process, your relationship has turned for the worse, and you have negative feelings toward your previous partner. Some time goes by and now you are faced with an opportunity for a new relationship. The major difference is now you carry the baggage from the previous relationship. How do you know that you are carrying baggage? It's simple. Listen to yourself talk, and the speech that you give to your friends. For example, you say "I've been done wrong before, and I don't want it to happen again." Let's explore where that leads us....

So, what do you do, when you have that statement as the headline of your new relationship? What kind of effect does that tone have on your behavior and the behavior of your partner? The first rule of the universe is whatever you put out, you get back. It has the same effect as the Biblical scripture of "you reap what you sew". This is how it plays out. You will go through your next relationship expecting to be treated in the same manner as you were treated in your previous or past relationship. Do you know what the consequences of that thought pattern are? You <u>will</u> receive the same treatment as you experienced before, creating a self-fulfilling prophecy. The reasons are the following: 1) self-sabotage, 2) refusal to evaluate the problems in your previous relationship, 3) refusal to evaluate your personality traits, 4) refusal to evaluate your previous partner's personality traits, and 5) pure negative expectations.

Let's start with negative expectations. If you don't expect anything, you won't receive anything. If you expect negative results, you will get negative results. Think about it this way. If in the back of your mind, you expect every person you meet to cheat on you, then you will end up with that type of partner. Our expectations can raise or lower our standard. If we have minimal expectations, then the candidate pool becomes bigger. We start accepting potential partners without being discerning (blind to the negative traits identified in previous partners) of who this person is and how they think. It is important when you meet people to have in your own mind the qualities of the partner that you <u>do want</u> instead of thinking of the qualities of a partner that you <u>don't want</u>. In that way, those positive qualities will stand out, when evaluating someone, and if those qualities are missing, you will notice that too. If the qualities are missing, then keep it moving. There is an idea spawned by philosopher Rene Descartes which denotes, [as a man thinks, so is he]. For the purpose of this chapter, the quote means that whatever you think about is what you gravitate towards. So, in the process of finding a partner, why would you ponder on the partner that you don't want causing yourself to attract the undesirable to you? That point also leads into self-sabotage. Attracting negative qualities because of low expectations and doubt in finding a suitable partner is an action of self-sabotage in itself.

Another way that we walk into negative relationships through self-sabotage is punishing the new person for actions that they didn't commit. I had a friend that said, "Trust has to be earned not given in a new relationship." I know that many of you think that on the surface this is a great idea, but in actuality, this is a negative concept and here is why. What this friend is really saying is the following, "I don't trust you and you have to continually pass tests until I believe that you have earned the right for me to trust you." The first problem with this statement is you will never be satisfied because the more you look for something, the more it appears. The tests that you devise will become more crazy, more challenging, and more impossible as time goes on. This is because, as people, we are insatiable, and there is no limit to what we imagine. You will even ask them to achieve tasks that you would fail yourself. Then, in the end, your irrational mind says when that person runs for the hills, "see, they didn't love me anyway." You are absolutely right, because the person that you put forth was not the real you. It was a demon, an evil manifestation, an insane person. Stop it. Stop the madness. Let me ask you a question, "Is that your idea of love? Is that what you think love really is? Is that how you think love should be demonstrated to you?" No. Since love is difficult to define and everyone shares their own beliefs on what love is, I will use the idea of love as explained by the Bible, so that we will have a common definition. In 1 Corinthians 13:4-8, it states, "Love suffers long and is kind; love does not envy; love does not parade itself, is not puffed up; does not behave rudely, does not seek its own, is not provoked, thinks no evil; does not rejoice in iniquity, but rejoices in the truth; bears all things, believes all things, hopes all things, endures all things. Love never fails." The purpose of this quote is for you to determine if you have conditional love for a person or unconditional love for a person. If your love is conditional, then this particular partner may be a temporary union for the purpose of learning a lesson or identifying your core needs. This may not be the partner for a lifetime, because if a particular condition of negativity presents itself, your "relationship" may end.

Side note: The previous scripture described love. It did not say "relationship". This means that your love for the person should survive whether you stayed in the relationship or not. How often do we continue to love a person when the relationship ends or the break up is bad? This is when we discover that we had conditional love for our previous partner. Many of us have come to the realization that we've been in conditional relationships-either we or our partner had conditions. This is fine. We will go through many conditional relationships as learning lessons to prepare us for the unconditional relationship. The real tragedy is when we bind ourselves to a conditional relationship, and give up on the idea that we can have a bond with someone that can stand the test of time.

If you should find yourself, unable to think positively about your current partner, then the real reason for your behavior and lack of trust may be because you are pushing the person away. If that is your goal, then consider ending your relationship. Instead, find someone that you are really interested in dating and try to develop a healthy relationship. A healthy relationship for longevity is a bond of unconditional love. But, how can you develop a healthy relationship, when you are sick yourself? That IS self-sabotage. One becomes sick when they are unable or unwilling to attempt to heal the parts of their past that negatively affect them, and are unwilling or unable to identify the negativity in their own thoughts and actions.

Leaving the Past in the Past: A New You for the Future

Referring to the earlier statement of not letting the past relationship "happen again", yes, you are right. Don't let that happen again! **But the behavior that has to change is YOURS, not the other persons.** Let me repeat that. THE BEHAVIOR THAT HAS TO CHANGE IS YOURS, NOT THE OTHER PERSONS. For example, I often hear this complaint, "I gave so much and didn't get anything in return." You are right, don't do that again. Why continue to give to a person that 1) does not want it or 2) does not respect it? This is where, being true to yourself, loving yourself, and respecting yourself comes in. If you give and get nothing in return, then stop giving. In the Bible, Matthew 7:6 states, "Do not give what is holy to the dogs; nor cast your pearls before swine, lest they trample them under their feet, and turn and tear you in pieces." Are you dating swine? If it is a continuous occurrence, then re-evaluate your purpose for being there. Some of us give our all in a relationship. That is fine. The problem comes when you have given all that you've got, with nothing in return. So, when you are empty and you need to be refilled, then what? Your relationship will start to wither, because you can no longer carry it. A relationship takes TWO. If you are giving your all, your partner has to give you their all, so that all bases will be covered. If they don't, you won't have anything left to give to them or yourself. If you give to them, and they give to themselves, who is giving to you? This is a one sided relationship. You are in that relationship by yourself. If you are dating yourself, what's the point of having someone else there? So, again, I have to ask this question. Why would you stay in a relationship where you are not being fulfilled? Change YOUR behavior. People can only do to you what you allow. Respect yourself and others will follow suit. If a person disrespects or undervalues you, then that is not the person for you. That is not a healthy union.

The basic point of this chapter is the only thing you should walk away with from a previous relationship is a clearer understanding of what you actually WANT in a relationship. Don't allow a previous relationship to cause you to be mentally, emotionally and physically unhealthy. Learn the lessons, discover the traits, and shake off all of the negativity. There is a Biblical principal of "everything that sets itself up for evil, will be turned around for my good." Romans 8:28 states, "And we know that all things work together for the good to those who love God, to those who are called according to His purpose." Adopt this perspective.

Side note: Everyone has a purpose in life. If negative things have happened to you and you did not die as a result of them, then that means that you have another chance to figure out and fulfill your purpose here on earth. We are all placed on this earth for a reason. Some of you think that your purpose is to be "so and so's" wife or husband. Not quite. We are all supposed to be working toward the greater good of mankind. So, figure out the reason for your presence here. Many times people are taken from this world when their purpose has been fulfilled or when they refuse to figure out what it is. It may be that in pursuit of this mission that you may find your better half. So, use a break-up for positivity instead of negativity.

Cutting Ties: Purposeful Separation vs. the Ripping Effect

Everyone cannot stay in your life, but the way that a person exits your life is up to you. This is a phenomenon that I like to call **Purposeful Separation vs. the Ripping Effect.**

"Purposeful Separation" is when you agree to split up. You have an understanding of the reasons why, and you accept the fact that the separation will occur. You prepare yourself for the removal of the thing that binds (attachment to and ease of familiarity with your current partner). Therefore, you are able to divide, leaving yourself in tact. When you REFUSE to look forward and acknowledge the time of separation, you continue to the era known as the "Ripping Effect".

The "Ripping Effect" is a form of separation that is very painful. Whether you are ripping yourself from someone or someone is ripping themselves from you, the result is still the same. This is because in the process of ripping you become separated from pieces of yourself. Ripping is not a "clean" procedure. Pieces of you remain on the person you were attached to and pieces of them remain attached to you as well. That is why it seems so hard to leave. Know and understand why the separation is necessary. It doesn't mean that you have to like it, but it is better when you have a rational perspective about why the separation is occurring.

For example, your partner tells you that they don't want to be in a relationship with you anymore. You have two options. One, you can accept that they want to leave and start the mental process of being without them. Two, you can deny the fact of their desire to exit and force the person to stay with you. Your partner already indicated that they wanted to leave. The more time that goes by, the more your partner wants to leave. Your partner is going to begin the process of "**Prying**" or "**Manipulative Separation**". This is when your partner starts acting in a way to persuade you by uncharacteristic behavior to now want to be out of the relationship. Their speech may become more "disrespectful" or they may stop talking altogether. Your partner may appear to care about your feelings less and less. They may move on to someone or something else while you are still attached. If there is a behavior that you can't stand, they will begin to perform those actions. Your partner is doing this out of frustration and out of the feeling of being bound, not because they don't love you. Now, you are in the position of compromising your desires and needs in order to make them stay. After some time, you will actually place yourself in a position to be abused. This "self-sacrifice" will not work for long, because everyone is true to themselves in the end. If you do not act in accordance with your needs, then it will be the beginning of the death of you (your soul, your hopes, your dreams, your desires, your happiness, your life-force).

When you have been released either through acknowledgement and acceptance or by ripping, the next phase is even more telling. What is the result after the division has taken place? A hole exists where the "adhesive" used to be. So, how are you going to plug that gaping space?

The answer depends on the person. Some people patch the hole with whatever they can find (i.e. alcohol, drugs, rebound, jump-off, immediate dates, bitterness, etc.) Some, when they notice a hole has developed, are overcome by a sense of fear and run back to attempt to reattach themselves to the piece that has already been separated. In this way, when the separation comes again, their hole is even bigger than the first one that they tried to plug. Those that attempt to reattach themselves will require major surgery.

Some use ointments, gauze, medication or stitches through religion, self-reflection, enlightenment, awakening to their goals and purpose, new perspectives on life and love, refocusing their attention towards the future in a positive way "now I have the chance to…" etc.) These menders move forward and trigger the process of regeneration, so that the evidence of the hole and the scar that covered it are barely noticeable after time.

The last group simply does nothing and bleeds out completely until death. Which will you choose?

Instead of saying "why did they leave?" Ask yourself, "Why were they here? What was their purpose in my life? What was I supposed to learn from this situation?

What am I supposed to see about MYSELF?" Remember, **start every relationship with positivity.**

"Without failure you would never know you were making the moves toward success."-Ocean Shaw

Chapter Five

FIGHTING FOR LOVE

"Knowing when to fight takes the same wisdom as knowing when to leave." -Ocean Shaw

"A smart man can make good decisions in the moment. A wise man can look ahead to make prosperous decisions for a lifetime." -Ocean Shaw

In the last chapter, we discussed the issue of break-ups. Now, I want to address the idea of fighting for love. If this is not your first relationship, you have been placed in a position where you or your partner had to determine whether to fight to stay together. Either you were the one fighting to save the relationship, or someone was fighting to keep you in the relationship. Whichever role you played, the decision to act may have been based on your motivation or lack thereof and prior experience. Motivation is oftentimes based on determining if the actions needed to obtain your goal are worth the effort. It is in the process of correctly or incorrectly evaluating a person's motivations or our own motivations that lead us to make faulty decisions. If you do not assess your true reason for remaining with someone, then you can make a choice that is detrimental to your happiness. For example, some of our motivations make us threaten to leave because we want to see if our partner really cares about us. Other motives for leaving a relationship may be due to boredom or unfulfillment.

Side note: Breaking up with someone to discover their true feelings is an erroneous tactic. First, don't bring up the idea of separation unless you really want that person to leave. Second, the way you can tell if a person really wants to be with you is how they treat you in the relationship.

In the alternative, a person's motives to remain in a relationship may be financial or because of fear or from just plain giving up. Other motives may be because they truly want to be in a relationship with you. Whatever the motive and whatever the reason, discovering the truth is your responsibility. If you were honest or in touch with your needs, sometimes you would realize that you were fighting for relationships that were counter-productive and lacking in the essentials to make the relationship work. So, in fighting for love or in deciding to stay, how can you discover the truth or make the best decision? First, be honest with yourself about what needs aren't being met. Second, be honest with yourself about your relationship and where it may be going-nowhere?

Some of you may be thinking of ending your relationship and don't know whether to stay and fight or to leave. Write down your complaints. Are they *deal breakers* or are you complaining about petty things? What is the major problem in your relationship? It is important to identify what you are displeased about, and also to evaluate your own behavior in the relationship. If your partner's issues are *deal breakers*, meaning you will not be able to live with these issues, then evaluate your purpose for being there. Think of why it may be worth it to continue in your relationship. If your partner's issues are petty things or issues that can be solved, then devise a plan to improve and communicate with your partner in order to strengthen the bond. The most unconstructive decision we can make is to complain to our family and friends about our partner's shortcomings, especially if we do not want out of the relationship. This decision is unconstructive because creating a negative outlook on your relationship for those closest to you will make those people seek to end your relationship, **so they can end your complaining**. Oftentimes, those closest to you will act in a way to bring about the end of your relationship. So, don't complain unless you want your relationship to be over.

Decided to Stay: Why Complain?

Sometimes we complain about our partner, because complaining is what we do best. If we were faced with the opportunity to leave, we wouldn't take it. Don't frustrate yourself and others around you. Before you open your mouth to complain, force yourself to say three positive things about your partner. If you still want to complain after that, change your thoughts. Instead of focusing on the negative traits of your partner, think of your partner's good attributes. Sometimes, the **focus** on negative behavior or petty quirks is what causes the rift in the relationship.

Complaining is more of a venting technique than an attempt to enrich and build up your relationship. What are the benefits of complaining? How does complaining improve your overall situation? We are all frustrated by people and disappointed in them from time to time, and this is understandable. However, we cannot stay in this state of frustration. It is important to address the problem with your partner in a loving way, not with anger and bitterness. Also, venting to others for the purpose of complaining about your partner, without looking for suggestions of improvement for you and your partner, only lead to you painting a negative picture of your partner to your family and friends. If you are going to remain in the relationship, then provide your family and friends with a positive outlook of your partner. Let everyone know, including yourself, why you want to be with your partner. Why would you continuously complain to your friends and family about your partner, and continue to stay in your relationship? Either, the people listening will no longer want to hear it or they will start to mistreat your partner and help you end your relationship.

Deciding to Leave?: Give It All You've Got

There are those of you who are SERIOUSLY considering leaving and don't know what to do. My first question to you is, "do you really want to try?" This is important because if you do not want to put any effort into making it work, and you do not have a firm decision to leave, then you can become complacent, remaining in your situation "just because". In this decision to be complacent, you may end up settling for mediocrity and boredom, with the only thing passing being time. Wasted time-time you could be dating, going on trips, trying a new hobby, meeting new friends, saving money, shopping, going to concerts or starting a business. It is your life and your decision. At the very least, fight for your own happiness.

For those who want to put in the effort and come to a firm decision, here are some options. First, try discussing your issues with your partner. Your approach will determine what kind of response you get. Find a good relaxing time to talk, where they may be open to listening. During the football game, may not be a good time. While your partner is trying to go to sleep, may not be a good time. Set up an event like a date, i.e. invite them to dinner. In discussing your issues, don't be accusatory, saying things like, "you don't do this and I don't like it; I think I want to leave". Start out telling them positive things that they are doing and break the issues to them in a caring way. For example, you can start with, "I could not have asked for a more dedicated partner in you. You have always given an effort to make sure that…. I was wondering if I could ask one more thing of you…." You should express yourself however you feel comfortable. You know your partner and what they respond to, these are just examples. Give them an opportunity to try to meet those needs. If you don't see any changes after that, remind them of your previous conversation and illustrate how important these things are to you. Give them a chance to improve. If that still doesn't work, then find out from them why they are unable to perform. These are just suggestions. The main point is to give your all to make the relationship work. If you have done everything you can do to no avail, then there are no regrets and you are able to leave with a clear conscience.

Some of you will say that my suggestion to talk your problems out with your partner is too much work. The result of not doing it that way is that you will find yourself going back and forth, and your relationship will not really be over. As soon as they say to you, "give us a chance, we haven't really tried to make this work", your guilt will kick in and you will go back anyway. Why waste time? In the alternative, you can end up having a bad break up and may get your tires slashed. It's never a good idea to "spring" a break up on anyone.

Choosing Between Two People: The Best Fit

Some of you are trying to make a choice between two people. What happens in this scenario is you can't continue to go between the two. Eventually, you have to make a choice, and now you have two people vying to be in a relationship with you. Normally the suitors have different personalities and you are trying to decide which one is best. Provided that the two suitors are displaying their TRUE personalities, the best way to judge is based on their behavior until this point. I am going to illustrate this point with an example to hopefully make the idea more clear.

One of the suitors has been there a little longer than the other. We will call the one with extended history, the "present partner". We will call the newer person, the "prospective partner". The following is the scenario that you can find yourself in.

The present partner has grown comfortable in the relationship and has slacked off in maintaining the bond. This has opened the door for you to become bored, and caused you to entertain the idea of meeting other people. You have met a prospective partner on the side. Time has gone by and now you have to make a choice between the present partner and the prospective partner. Most people know that the other person in the relationship is starting to stray, whether they admit it or not. What normally happens is one of the suitors starts fighting very furiously to keep their position, and the other suitor seems to be hanging back. People normally go for the person that is fighting the strongest. I want to offer the idea that choosing who to stay with based on how hard that person is fighting may be a little short-sighted. Thinking that the person who is fighting more has more love can be erroneous. **You have to determine their motivation for fighting.** It may be possible that the true fighter for your love is the person that is putting up the least resistance. I will explain in the following paragraphs.

The determination of the true fighter for your love is where I want to alter your perspective. The true fight for your love does not occur when a person caters to your needs for a short time or when a threat to end the relationship is near. A **true fight** is when someone tries to meet your needs on a DAILY basis. The person that shows their love for you shows a dedication to you. This person wants to make you happy and wants to do the things you like. It is not a job for them to please you or to consider your wants and desires. Now, some may have more time invested, but their complete dedication (desire to fulfill your needs and wants) to you was only for securing the relationship and not for maintaining the bond.

Determining Motivation: Why Fight?

For those who have slacked on the job and are now fighting furiously, what is their motivation? What are they fighting against? Abandonment? Loneliness? Separation? Being Single? Tell me which one of those motives have to do with YOUR needs or YOUR happiness. If these are examples of their motives, then they are not fighting for your love. The result is going to be that they will do what is required for a little while and then go back to slacking. This is because the motive was to keep you from leaving, and not to maintain the relationship. Some of you are rewarding short term fervent fights rather than the person who fought for your love every day. Consider this. The person who is putting up the more active fight has the energy to wage a short term forceful battle for you, because they haven't put in the effort all of this time to keep you. The one who has put in the effort every day, however, doesn't appear to be fighting because they have spent their energy daily to maintain the relationship. In their eyes (the person "not fighting"), it appears that after all of their striving, you still want to leave or you still aren't convinced that you want to be in a relationship. Their question to you is, "fight for what?" This person has given you their all. There is nothing else they can do. Their statement to you is, "I have given you 100% and you still want something else. If that is the case, then you should go." In their minds, they cannot satisfy you, so they will let you go.

Some of you are being lead astray by the fervent warfare and are missing out on the true winner. You know that you have been misled about a person's true intentions for remaining in the relationship, when you find yourself in the same position as when you started, but with your "real" relationship ruined. Then you find yourself wanting to rekindle the relationship of the person you let go. Please learn by wisdom and not experience. Don't let the opportunity to have your "best" relationship, pass you by because you inaccurately judge situations. They may take you back, but there are some things that aren't repairable.

If you are considering leaving, make it clear to yourself why you desire to be out of that relationship. Ask yourself, "Why am I leaving? Why isn't it working out? What is my purpose for remaining in this relationship?" If you are attempting to decide between two suitors, then evaluate what kind of relationship you really want, and who would be the person to provide that atmosphere. Motivation is a strong force that pushes people into action. The most important lesson we can learn is how to determine what motivates people into action, and is that motive in my best interest? **Every decision we make not only affects our present, but also our future.**

Chapter Six

DO YOU NEED A TRANSLATOR?

"Our lives begin to end the day we become silent about things that matter."   -Dr. Martin Luther King, Jr.

Most people communicate their needs. The question is "are you listening?" For some people, their significant other's infidelity or desire for separation comes as a shock. Why? Usually it entails at least one of these following reasons: 1) you were not listening; 2) you are selfish and only concerned with your own needs and wants; or finally 3) you don't understand your partner when they communicate.

How can any of these scenarios happen to you? First, you tune out your partner when it sounds like they are complaining. You think "Awh! I don't want to hear that mess!" or "Don't bring me any negativity." Just because you ignore the problem doesn't mean that the problem goes away. Why are you so reluctant to hear your partner's issues? Is it because you don't want to acknowledge that your partner is not satisfied? Do you feel that you cannot satisfy your partner? Do you feel as if you have given your all? Are you unwilling to do more? Do you think that your partner is unreasonable? These are valid concerns, if you have them, but what these concerns point to is an unbalanced union. The minute that you are reluctant to hear and address your partner's concerns, you open the door in your relationship to separation. If you were interested in maintaining your relationship, you would do whatever it takes to keep it alive. So, what could your actions be saying about the issues in your relationship? How can your actions feed into and perpetuate the above concerns? If the request of your partner causes you to have to consciously perform in order for your partner to be satisfied, then their needs may be outside of your constant state of being. What does this mean? It means that you have to become someone else in order for your partner to be satisfied. This is where being honest about the consistent and real you are important in the advent of dating. (True to yourself is acting in accordance with your needs and desires.) For example, if your deal breaker is dishes in the sink, and your partner could care less about dishes in the sink, then what do you always seem to be fighting about? Let me guess, dishes in the sink. There's someone out there that loves a clean kitchen, just like you. That frees you up to argue about other things, but nothing that causes you to look at your partner differently.

Relationship Style: Actions Communicate Needs

It is important to identify what type of relationship you need. Do you need a partner? A partner bond is a relationship where you and your significant other participate in activities together. This means that it is important for you to share the same interests and to enjoy spending a lot of time together. Do you need a gender opposite? A gender opposite bond is a relationship where you and your significant other participate in activities separately. The majority of your time is engaged in your separate interests and you come together for social events and dinner. In turn, you may like the idea that your partner has separate friends and a separate itinerary.

Failure to identify your relationship style can lead to problems down the road. To further illustrate this point, the following paragraphs will explain someone who needs a "partner bond". For example, you like to go out. Your partner would rather stay home. You are always saying, "take me out. Let's do something tonight." Your partner says, "go on honey. Have a great time." You have two choices. One choice is you can stay home, but you will be disappointed and frustrated. The second choice is you can go out. There is nothing inherently wrong with the second choice. But the question I have is what happens when you and your partner start to lead separate lives? What happens when you meet someone, while you are out, that loves the same things you do? What happens when the opportunity arises for you and your new friend to share these activities together? The only point that I am making is that it may be stronger for your relationship, if you can share the same interests. This may help to eliminate the occurrence of infidelity. There are all sorts of reasons that can cause someone to go outside of the relationship. However, some people don't step outside of the relationship because they don't love you. Some people step outside of the relationship because they are unfulfilled.

Let's continue with this point of being in a relationship with someone that has different expectations and needs. Some of you may say that sharing your interests with someone other than your significant other doesn't always have to lead to infidelity. I agree. If you need someone to do things with or someone that shares the same interests, what happens to this need when your partner doesn't fulfill it and your new friend does? Won't the new bond with someone else put a strain on your current relationship? Well, you can deny your true self for a little while, but that does not carry the trappings for success over the long run for your current relationship. Your significant other is either going to have to become what you need, or you may be tempted to stray. Discover what relationship style you need upfront, so that you will not be confronted with the desire to stray later.

In the alternative, you forego your needs and instead adopt your significant other's passions. For example (using the same scenario as above) instead of going out like you prefer, you stay home and sit on the couch. How long will it take for you to become weary of acting? In other words, how long can you keep up this new behavior? One week? A month? A year? Why go through all of that, when you can acknowledge your limits, your comfort level, your desires, your needs in the beginning, and find someone who loves you for exactly who you are, not the person you've created. I will admit that relationships take work, but some of you are working at EVERY level. You can't keep that up for seventy years. You are going to get tired. For instance, it is tough to work together towards a common goal, to communicate about feelings and events, to coordinate schedules, families, children, and work. Why would you want to add inventing a personality to the list? That seems very difficult and trying, but if you want to do that, it is your choice. To each his or her own!

Communication Meltdown: What Do You Mean?

What happens when the communication is unclear? This means that you have no idea what your partner is talking about or you are saying everything else except what is important. Your relationship may be experiencing a communication meltdown. Somehow, your or your partner's needs are not being expressed clearly or effectively or in the worst case, those needs are not being communicated at all. How does your partner communicate currently?

- Do they need time to think about what you've said and return to you later with a response?
- Do they tell you how they're feeling through actions, i.e. storming out, throwing things, crying, silent treatment?
- Does your partner attempt to persuade using punishment and withdrawal, i.e. no sex, no dinner, no phone calls, not coming home?
- Do they speak in riddles, parables or words you don't have the meaning for?
- Do they use criticism and sarcasm to make their point?
- Is everything a joke?
- Do they just agree with everything you say and offer no input or ideas?

- Is your partner blunt, direct, and to the point or do they talk around an issue and never express a main point?
- Do they keep bringing up the same issue day after day or talk about it incessantly?
- Does your partner provide excuses for everything?
- Do they point out all of your faults during an argument?
- Do they not speak at all or give one word responses?

Now, think about a style of speech either represented above, or one you devise on your own that will allow you to focus on and understand what your partner is saying. For example, if your mind tends to wander, do you need someone that gets to the point? Or if you are sensitive, do you need someone to "sugar coat" their message? We all respond differently to information, and we all process language in a different fashion. Based on our personalities and experiences, some manners of speaking turn us off, make us bored, or irritate and anger us. Determine which communication style will best fit you and allow you to speak with and understand your partner better.

What happens when your partner is listening, but what you're saying is foolishness? Women and insecure individuals are mainly guilty of this. For some of you, it is better that your partner ignores you, in order to save you from yourself. Here are some examples. "I need some personal space", when you really meant to say, "I want more attention." Why is this foolish? It is foolish, because once you are given your personal space, you are upset that they did not run after you to invade your "personal space", when you asked for "personal space". That is not the way to communicate that you are insecure about their feelings for you. The way to communicate your insecurity is to say, how do you feel about me and then express why you have doubts. Another example is "since you keep looking at them, why don't you go over there and introduce yourself?" What you really mean to say is, "what is it about them that really catches your attention?"

Side note: People, let's get real. For men, she has a really big booty or big breasts, whatever he likes. You know your man. He is having his three second fantasy, but he isn't leaving you. Don't be so insecure. Some people cheat because their sense of value and worth of the relationship has decreased. Some people cheat according to convenience. For example, he is going to cheat with someone that gave him an almost guarantee of the vagina or because of an emotional attachment. In the case of an emotional attachment, there are major issues in your relationship and maybe you should be worried. But that person is normally not the person you see haphazardly in the street.

The last thing that you want your partner to do is to go over there and introduce themselves. So why offer that as an option? You haven't met the person that would actually listen to you, and go over there. Because if you had, I'm sure that you would be cured of that statement. The moral of the story is, say what you mean.

Words said out of spite and anger also fall into the category of foolishness. For example, "I should have been with your brother or sister." Utter foolishness. "I'm only with you for the money." "I just wanted my kids to look like you." **If you have the opportunity to express yourself, then use it wisely.** The funny thing about words is that they can act like a recording, especially when negative. Words play in the hearer's head over and over again, recreating negative feelings toward the person who spoke them. So, if you aren't interested in a separation, wouldn't you rather your partner ponder on ideas that will positively affect your relationship? Why tear a person down and expect to be in a healthy union with them? You are sabotaging your relationship, and making it so that you are the only person who desires to continue the bond. What kind of effect do you think carrying dead weight is going to have on your forward movement? Remove emotions and use logic when speaking, if you are unable to communicate in a positive manner.

Positive Reinforcement: Honey not Vinegar

If a person wants to be with you, then compliment them on the areas where they are succeeding and encourage them to expand in the areas where they are lacking. This only works if they have a desire to please you. For example, if the issue is you aren't getting enough attention, then say, "I love it when you look at me when I enter the room. I feel like the most beautiful person in the world." If you like a certain dish, what is the point in saying, "You never cook steak!" No, try saying, "I love it when you prepare steak. It's the best steak I've tasted in a long time." (Men, don't add-"almost like my mama's".   That comment brings insecurity.) Again, this is helpful when your partner wants to please you. **This is the key.** Some of you have partners that are high maintenance, spoiled, selfish, and unyielding. If your partner had the answer to cracking the SAT, then no one would go to college.

Power of Persuasion: Only by Listening

When we speak in terms of communication our first thought goes to the act of speaking. However, one of the most important aspects of communication is listening. Listening is the greatest tool for discovering information. It is when we listen to others and allow them to fully express their ideas, we can learn a lot about how they think and reason. Whenever we find ourselves in a conversation with someone, especially an argument, often we find ourselves thinking of what we are going to say, rather than listening to what the other person is saying. We can be so anxious to make our point or solely focused on "winning" that we ignore the other person's point of view. There is no prize in "winning" an argument (making the other person become silent). There is only a benefit to getting the other person to understand your point of view and in understanding their interpretation of events. This can only be achieved by listening. How can you persuade a person to your side of the argument if you do not listen to why they are opposed to your view? Listening will allow you to communicate more effectively by understanding your partner. Understanding your partner means that you are aware of what they need to hear (what their needs are) and how you need to say it (what form of speech will allow your information to register). Remember, we can learn from anyone, but it is hard to learn while talking.

Side note: This is for all of the stalkers and super-sleuths out there. Listening is better than checking cell phones, bank accounts, and underwear. Listening is better than sitting outside of your partner's house or following them to work. Ask your partner about their day, then shut up. No, I mean shut up for a while. Allow awkward silence to set in. In some cases, this gives them time to relax and unwind. After awhile, most people start talking. They start talking about whatever, but there is crucial information in there. People talk about what they see everyday or their experiences. Most people want to talk about it, so why not have your partner feel comfortable discussing their experiences with you? The crucial information will come out, the more comfortable your partner gets. When you hear it, don't address it. Most people tell on themselves. Just wait. For more on that and other techniques, see my upcoming book, "Whatever the hell else I come up with" in stores near you! But, if you have a non-talker, then consider stalking or a low jack or something, because you are out of luck on the conversation side....

Chapter Seven

APPETITE FOR SEX

"Nothing makes you forget about love like sex." –Staci Beasley

Sex is one of the many topics that people don't want to discuss, but it is one of the main reasons for breakups in relationships. A lack of sexual compatibility can send a relationship on an endless downward spiral and open the door to additional complications, i.e. infidelity and a lack of intimacy in the relationship. This is a topic where you definitely have to be honest with yourself about what your sexual needs entail. Sex is a topic where philosophy does not always agree with action. Many say that sex is supposed to be reserved for marriage, but a virgin at the altar nowadays is as rare as a comet hitting the earth, it's not impossible, but it is not a common occurrence. So, since many people are "practicing" for marriage, we should be able to put philosophy and ideology to the side. This will allow us to be open and honest about what we like and don't like in the bedroom, as well as address some outside issues that affect the ability to create intimacy within the bedroom. For example, if we are "practicing" for marriage, why does the sex seem to cease after marriage? What causes us to lose our affinity for sex in long term relationships? One of the reasons for the loss of intimacy is because we turn a blind eye to sexual compatibility in the evaluation of our prospective partners.

Compatibility

Just as our core beings display personality, so do our sexual tendencies. This means that everyone has a "sexual personality". What we like and how we express ourselves in the bedroom varies from person to person. While we have a list or thought about the general qualities that we desire in our mates, sometimes we assume that sex will work itself out in the relationship. Au contraire! Our thoughts, perceptions, expectations, and even past experiences are all brought into the bedroom with us as we attempt to negotiate the act of sex. Meaning, what we are willing to do sexually is determined based on our ideas of who we are, what we are supposed to be, and how these previous factors tie into our identities. For example, if oral sex requires you to get on your knees or place yourself in the subservient position, and in your mind, you don't bow down to anyone, then you may be apprehensive in performing oral sex. Everything in our being is connected and oftentimes, we cannot turn that off. Another example is some men believe that to have feelings and to show sensitivity is a sign of weakness. So, in the sexual escapades of a man who holds this belief, we may see him perform hard pounding sex with little intimate behavior (kissing or touching), and then when he is finished, put his clothes on and leave without further comment. This example, along with the previous example, are reasons to look for sexual compatibility in our partners. In the area of sexual compatibility, both men and women need to be honest with themselves, not only in the physical realm, but also with their psychological needs as well. Men should be honest about their expectations, and women should provide a realistic demonstration of how far they are willing to go.

Misrepresentations

Sex is an area where there is a lot of misrepresentation, and often it is the women who are blamed for doing it. How are people misrepresenting themselves? Here are some examples: you will do anything just to get the person to stay in a relationship with you. The truth is you don't want to "give head" (for those who are still uneasy with sexuality-fellatio or cunnilingus). You pretend to have a high sex drive when you really don't. The truth is you really only want to have sex once a month. You buy sexy lingerie and heels. The truth is you would rather wear your pajamas, and lingerie is only for extremely special situations, like once every three years. You profess to be able to go for hours. The truth is that you are lazy and you only have a good 15 minutes before you give out. You profess to know what women need. The truth is you don't know where to begin to find the G spot. You start out romantic and thoughtful. The truth is foreplay is actually you thinking about having sex, not actually performing it. Additionally, the truth is you are allergic to restaurants, movies, trips or anything that involves money. There is someone out there that is just as restrained or open-minded as you. There are people who place value and importance on the same things you do such as, holidays, birthdays, dating, and gifts. Figure out what your needs and requirements are and align yourself with them. You do not have to settle nor do you have to force someone to adopt your sexual personality. Sex should be a free flowing and enjoyable experience, not a prison term.

How do you know that someone has misrepresented their sexual personality? There is an old school saying, "how you get them is how you keep them." Very simple, but very profound. In other words, the behavior that encouraged you to pursue a relationship disappears. Whatever behavior you engaged in to secure a person's interest is the same behavior that will be required to maintain that person's interest. If you begin the dating relationship giving your partner sex whenever they wanted it, then in your "monogamous" relationship you will have to continue giving your partner sex whenever they want it. If you begin the dating relationship buying flowers and going to nice restaurants, then you will have to continue that behavior for the duration of your partnership. If you start out giving head and doing all sorts of freaky things, then your partner will expect that same behavior once your relationship is official. Instead of putting your best foot forward, put your real foot forward and find a partner who is satisfied with your level of sexual commitment. Meaning, act in accordance with your needs and desires in the beginning, so you can find a partner that is sexually compatible.

In order to look at compatibility and truthful representations in a more tangible way, I have devised some questions to get you thinking. I cannot provide specific answers because I am not you. All I can do is ask questions to get you thinking about what you like and require in the bedroom. There is no uniform answer as we are all different. When determining your sexual personality, consider these general questions before delving into more specific preferences. Seek to discover your fundamental traits.

- How are you sexually? (Try anything once or already familiar with positions and styles you like.)
- How are you romantically? (Do you need romance or do you want to get straight down to business?)
- What are your expectations? (Will certain positions make you a whore? Or do notions of respect and judgment have no place in the bedroom?)

The following will be a list of questions geared toward helping you realize what you need for intimacy and all around good sex. Remember, you are contemplating spending the rest of your life with this person. Be honest. All guys are not sex fiends, and all women aren't prudes. What are you?

Do you have prudish tendencies?

- Does sweaty sex repulse you?
- Are you turned off by sweat dripping on you during intercourse?
- Is missionary the only acceptable position?
- Is "doggy-style" disrespectful to you?
- Is "head" out of the question?

- Will you only perform "head" as a reward for good behavior?

- Are dinner and a movie a prerequisite for sex?

- Do you think that someone who is sexually expressive is a poor representative for a parent? For example, if a woman wants to have a stripper pole installed in the basement, do you think that she will be a poor example for your daughter?

- Do you not discuss sex because it is bad manners and etiquette?

- Do the lights have to be completely off?

Do you have freakish tendencises?

- Are you willing to try anything once?

- Do you want to invent positions?

- Is video taping optional?

- Are the partners optional?

- Is the wetter the bed the better?

- Do you like to introduce toys?

- Are the only parts you haven't put your mouth on, internal organs?

Do you have exhibitionist tendencies?

- Does the possibility of getting caught make you more excited?

- Do you walk around naked?

- With the blinds drawn?

- And the light on?

- Do you get more aroused by sex in public places?

What kind of sex drive do you have?

- Do you only want to have sex once a week?

- Once a month? Everyday? Once a year? Never?

- Will you have sex with your friends and family in the house? Your children?

- Will you go home for lunch to have sex?

- Will you shut your office door and get a quickie?

- Does someone have to get you in the mood in order for you to be stimulated?

- Are you clitorally stimulated?

- Are you stimulated by penetration?

- Does the vagina have to be overflowing or does it have to be just wet enough for you to get your penis inside, because you like it super tight?

What size is your vagina? What size is your penis? Be honest. The statement "Size matters" is true. The statement "the bigger the better is often false." Not all vaginas can take all size penises, which is why penises come in different sizes. Some women cannot take a penis larger than seven inches. Some women need eight and larger to realize that they are having sex. Find the size that gives you the most pleasure and comfort. If the penis is too large, you will push him off of you or try to hold him back from full penetration or be reluctant to try different positions. This leaves your partner frustrated and dissatisfied, and thinking about calling someone "deeper" on the side. If the penis is too small, you will find yourself balancing your checkbook. This leaves you frustrated and dissatisfied, and thinking about calling someone "bigger" or trying a toy on the side. Why live your life like that? Be honest and get what you need.

How do you like it?

- Do you want it slow and steady?

- Do you want to start off slow and then pound away in the end?

- Do you want to be pounded from the start?

- Do you want your partner to kiss you during sex?

- Do you want to control the positions and the process?

- Do you want to be put up against the wall? On the counter? On the sink?

- Do you want to have sex in the shower?

- Do you want to alternate between head and sex all night?

- Do you want to be flipped and tossed about?

- Can you be woken up from your sleep to have sex?

- Is it better in the morning?

- Do you want to be woken up with head?

- Do you have to have candles? Music playing? Special song? Rose petals?

- Do you have to shower before sex? After sex?

- Do you like to role play?

- Do you like to dress up? Spanking? Whips? Chains?

- Will you participate in a threesome?

- Do you want your partner to talk during sex? Scream? Call your name?

Desire or Aversion: Acknowledging Physical Attraction

When determining who you are sexually, identify your limits. Some limits have nothing to do with the act of sex. Some limits have to do with the arousal to get you in the mood for sex. Again, you should be honest. If you have an aversion to a larger person, then be with someone smaller.

58

If you need a partner with a certain breast size, then get that or someone who is willing to undergo surgery. Appearance is important when we speak of attraction. This is one of the most superficial aspects of our being, but very determinative. Also consider long term effects. None of us physically stay the same throughout the years. So consider what your physical *deal breakers* are. For example, your partner may be the perfect size now, but after a few children or a few good meals, that could all change. Look ahead to ponder the possibility of still being attracted to your partner. Nothing is guaranteed, but a lot can be helped with earlier consideration.

Remember, be true to yourself (act in accordance with your needs). Don't try to bring someone up to your level sexually, or in the alternative down to your level. It won't last. That person cannot maintain a false desire or lack of a desire for sex. Sex is one of the most personally motivated acts of our being. **In order to have good sex, your partner has to desire you**. They have to want to please you and get pleasure out of the act themselves. Don't force it. Instead, involve yourself with a person that has a similar sex drive to yours and similar ideas of what is acceptable.

For the Virgins Out There

I know you will go through this chapter and say, what about me? I don't know what I like yet. It will be hard to determine compatibility. As far as knowing what to do, use your imagination. That is what experienced people do and don't do. Even if you have been having sex for a while, it can be awkward having sex with a person for the first time, because you are not familiar with their body or their likes or dislikes. At that point, you are on even keel. It takes time to learn someone. Although some have instant connections with partners, this is not guaranteed. If you want some practical advice, here it is. You don't have to have sex to figure it out. Ladies, if you want to know if you will like "giving head" (fellatio), then practice on a banana. Do it everyday to see if you would get tired. Perform neck exercises. Put your hand up to your mouth as if you are going to cough, now cough. Replicate the motion without coughing. See how long you can last on the fruit, before your mouth starts to lock up. Don't let your teeth scrub against the banana. For added effect, water down some pudding.

Gentlemen, if you want to know if you will like "giving head" (cunnilingus), then cut open a peach. Do it everyday to see if you would get tired. Perform tongue exercises. Try to lick all of the sides inside of the peach-slow, fast, around, flickering. See how long you can last, before your tongue looses elasticity. For added practice, slurp some soup, practice on an ice cream cone. Now to address the psychological effects of cunnilingus, do you have a problem with suffocation? If you do, you probably won't want to do it.

In all seriousness, look for the emotional aspects since you don't know. Emotions and mental perceptions are a big part of sex. What kind of mental and emotional state a person is in determines what kind of sex the person will have. For example, if you could care less about the person, and all you want to do is have sex, you may not do what it takes to please them and only be concerned with pleasing yourself. If you aren't attracted to the person, then you may not make any effort at all. If you are in love with the person, then you will want to do anything and everything to make sure that person will pass out at the end. So depending on how much of your emotional needs are met and how you think the person feels about you, then you can work on what you like later because that person will want to make sure you are satisfied and comfortable. They will try things to please you and be patient until you figure out what that is.

Psychological and Mental Effects of Sex

As I said earlier, sex involves every aspect of your being whether you'd like to admit it or not. We all enter sex with our own ideas of how we'd like to experience it, even if the motivations are selfish. Even if you attempt to turn off your emotions, before, during, or after sex, you have to bring yourself to the point of not having a feeling about the person at all, and even this is impossible. No matter the thought, there is always a feeling attached to it, i.e. happiness, sadness, euphoria, nonchalance, or anger. Your prior experiences also bring expectations to the bedroom or we may subconsciously compare our previous partners and situations when confronted with sexual activity. This is all before we've touched each other. Since our world is so sex-crazied, the value and beauty in sex has been diminished. If we treat sex as if the other person involved and the act of sex itself mean nothing, then this thought process can leave a lot of people with hurt feelings, low self-esteem, or a complete denial of emotion altogether when it comes to sex. It is important to take an honest look at the act of sex when we trivialize its meanings and effects. I would like for you to consider what you can do to yourself or to other people when you use sex in a careless way. This may shed some light on why some of your partners or even you, yourself, are having difficulty in the bedroom.

Many of you who cannot call yourselves virgins at the time of reading this book, can say that you are not in a relationship currently with the first person you've had sex with. Some of you can say that you know all too well the symptoms and mental strains of contracting a sexually transmitted disease. There are still some of you yet, who have had a child by someone you wish you could forget. Many of you can recall the feelings of being used by someone who did not care for you, but had no problem accepting your body as a gift or in exchange for payment. All of these statements and experiences create a mental baggage that has to be dealt with, and occurring all because of one simple act--**sex**.

Many of you have given yourself, at least once, to someone that did not respect you and with each time of doing so, you have lost a little bit of yourself. Some people will encourage you to have sex and tell you that it doesn't matter one way or the other. That is a person that doesn't value themselves highly and assigns little worth to their person. Sex is one of the few acts where we give someone our "self". It is also one of the acts where after we have given our-selves to someone, we have found our-selves "returned". Ask your friends how many of them are with the person that they first had sex with? How about the second? Or the twentieth? Are they with anyone now? How many of them want to be with the last person they had sex with? What about you? The answers to those questions can be very painful. Considering the present, when you meet the "love of your life", what number will they be? For some women, the man is the 40th, and for some men, she is the 235th-talk about used! Let's make an effort to see our bodies as more

---

Side note: I do not advocate asking your partner what number you are. **This can break up your relationship** if you are not willing to be honest and realize that you would not have any numbers if someone did not sleep with you. A person's number may be high or low based on their past and how they viewed themselves. A lot of us make mistakes or come to a new realization after maturity sets in, so let's not be judgmental. I am writing this passage in an effort for people to assign more value and worth to sex, to their bodies and more importantly to themselves. Our bodies are a precious gift and not a wash rag to be used over and over.

---

than just conduits to a fleeting feeling. The feeling is "fleeting" because without the other attachments i.e. a feeling of commitment, love, responsibility, care, and respect, it is just a moment of "ecstasy". In thinking about sex, the most important thing to consider is what you will feel when you come down.

If sex was fulfilling, then people wouldn't feel the constant need to have it all the time. Have you ever walked up to someone and said, "would you like some sex", and they replied, "I'm good. I already had that." Not often. Once we have sex, it seems as if we become slaves to it. It doesn't take much to convince us to do it, and any touch or comment can put us back in the saddle again. Sometimes we even have sex with people we can't stand, just because we want to have the feeling back. The ecstasy from sex leaves so fast, that you may get more enjoyment out of smoking crack. At least if you are going to give yourself to a person, why not choose a person that loves and respects you for who you are? This can lessen the emotional and mental baggage. It is more fulfilling to give yourself to someone who is willing to make a commitment to you, not just in words, but in deeds and emotions and thoughts. **You are your most precious commodity**. Why sell yourself short for a feeling that lasts even shorter and a person's departure that comes even faster? However, <u>what will last</u> is the feeling of being rejected, of being used, of not being wanted, of not being respected, of being undervalued, and <u>not being loved.</u>

Chapter Eight

MAINTENANCE

"When your image improves, your performance improves." -Zig Ziglar

"The greatest single cause of a poor self-image is the absence of unconditional love." -Zig Ziglar

Maintenance is a concept that I would like to leave with you as a very important reminder. Starting a relationship is easy, maintaining a relationship is the hard part. I have seen too many people do everything they can to be in a relationship, and then once a partner is acquired, the same people bail on the maintenance of the relationship. Your mere presence is not enough to keep the relationship going, neither is a mere statement of commitment. **The truth is you have them TODAY. It is up to you whether you have them TOMORROW.**

Always remember that a RELATIONSHIP IS A LIFE. It is a living, growing and breathing entity. It is a shame that some of you have been together with your partner for example ten years, and your relationship is only two years old because after two years of being together, you stopped putting forth an effort to keep it alive.

There are two important factors that require maintenance when involved in a relationship. The first factor is your physical appearance. The second factor is the relationship itself. Both are necessary for your connection's longevity. It is when we allow the spark and spontaneity to die in our connection with each other, that we become bored or restless in our relationships. There is always something

64

you can do. If you find yourself getting bored, then you should instigate the action. If there was something that the two of you used to participate in, and you stopped, then restart that activity. Do something out of the normal day to day in order to bring excitement to each other again. Whether it is helping out with the chores, introducing sex again, or changing your appearance, find a way to peak your partner's interest again. Perform these activities often. Sometimes we wait too late to try to spark our partner's interest and by the time, we decide to try something new, our · efforts are ill-received.

Why do people get into relationships and let themselves go? Imagine letting yourself go personally. Stop eating even though you know you are hungry. Stop going to the bathroom, or better yet, wet yourself. Don't wash, don't shave, don't do anything to better yourself. Now, tell me how long you can live like that, and how long will a person want to be with you under those conditions? Just as we make an effort to maintain our bodies, we should make an effort to maintain our relationships.

From now on, every time you take a step or make an effort to take care of yourself, do something to take care of your relationship. Every time you stop to eat, feed your relationship. Every time you shower or bathe, do something to clean up your relationship. Every time you go to the bathroom, do something to relieve your partner of a burden in the relationship. Just as we are forced to perform natural functions, we should also be compelled to take care of our intimate bonds and our appearance.

Physical Maintenance: How Do You Feel?

The attraction that normally leads us into romantic relationships starts with the outward appearance. After that, there is an added benefit to discover that our personalities are compatible. Over time, we become used to the physical features of our partner, and we begin to settle into our relationships. However, our physical appearance does not remain the same and with the passage of time, we all begin to age and change. Aging is inevitable, but how drastically we change is up to us.

Physical Health

Be honest with yourself. Look at your gene pool. Look at your parents and family members. Are they overweight? What do you need to do to maintain your appearance? Go to the gym? Continue to participate in fitness activities? Change what you eat? Take a dance class? Take up a sport? For some of you, it is okay to be a little overweight, but maintain your appearance. Think about your family histories. Did someone pass away due to high blood pressure, diabetes, stoke, heart disease, Alzheimer's Disease, cancer? Get tested early. Find a way to relax and meditate in order to reduce stress. Let go of a lot of baggage in your life, so that you can maintain good mental health. Increase activities that make you happy or content. Remember, life goes on whether you are here to enjoy it or not. Don't take work so seriously, because if you die, they will just hire someone else. Maintain your personal health (physical and mental) at all times.

Side note: Try to remain as healthy as possible, so as not to create an additional burden on your family. Healthcare is expensive and frequent or extended stays at the hospital are very costly. Limit the strain that you place on your relationship.

Personal Appearance

Again, maintain your appearance. Get your hair done, treat yourself to clothes or shoes every once and a while. Do something for yourself that makes you happy. It is good for a relationship when the partners are happy. This was geared mainly for the women.

Since the previous example may resonate more with women, men also have a responsibility to maintain their physical appearance. For example, look around at the men with extending beer bellies and receding hairlines. Women would like to have something nice to look at as well. So what do you need to do to maintain your appearance? It's okay if you want to have a beer or three, but you don't have to be a glutton. Eat a balanced meal, vegetables are okay. Go to the gym, tone up what you already have. Play sports if you are inclined. It is good for your stress and gives you ways to build up confidence. It also gives you the space you might desperately need. Our country is moving forward scientifically by leaps and bounds. You can get hair treatment. Don't be offended, instead utilize things that make you feel good about who you are and how you look.

Your appearance is not just for you. Your appearance is for your partner as well. You will get older, but get older gracefully. Participate in practices that maintain your attraction level to your partner. Don't let go of yourself.

Maintaining Your Connection: Where's the Spark?

In addition to maintaining your physical appearance, maintain the ACTUAL relationship. Each person should shoulder some of the responsibilities in the relationship, so that one partner doesn't get overwhelmed. The feeling of doing too much is what contributes to people's lack of desire to maintain their appearance. If your partner is tired and just wants to crash, then there won't be any sex. Do you want to have sex? Then do the dishes; get the children ready in the morning or for bed at night; fill up the gas tank of your partner's car the night before, so they don't rush out early in the morning; clean a room in the house. The less your partner has to do, the more they can relax and give you what you want.

Ladies, do you want him to desire you? Don't nag. Tell him what you want and allow him to do it. Develop patience. Constant reminding does not get the job done any faster. Instead, try building him up. **Let him know that you appreciate him for what he has already done.** If it is something minor, then do it yourself. If he feels as though he is making a contribution to the family, then that will inspire him to do more. Inspire your partner into action!

Why is the Fire Out?: Lack of Motivation

Inspiration is actually a good principal for maintenance. For some of you, the idea of maintenance inspires the same feelings as the idea of getting a root canal. It is hard to want to do something special for a partner that you can't stand. However, if your partner believed in you and showed you great love and support, then doing things to strengthen your relationship would come naturally, and you would be happy to perform those tasks. What many relationships lack is the desire to do anything extra. For some reason or another, people are not inspired by their partners. Without inspiration, there is no motivation. Without motivation, there is no action when it comes to relationships.

When choosing a partner, choose a partner that inspires you. Choose a partner that inspires you to be the greatest person that you can be. Select a partner that celebrates all of the good aspects of you. If you are with someone and you forget that you have good qualities, then you are not inspired. <u>Find a partner that thinks you are successful, even when you fail.</u> If you are inspired by your partner, it will be easy to maintain the relationship. <u>Enter into a relationship with someone that you BELIEVE in.</u>

"Before you can inspire with emotion, you must be swamped with it yourself. Before you can move their tears, your own must flow. To convince them, you must yourself believe." Winston Churchill

Chapter Nine

COMPROMISE

"Nowadays, men would rather be the king of mud, than be the king of brick, just as long as they can call themselves king."- Ocean Shaw

This chapter is for the strong women who will get to the end of this book, figure out who they are, and realize that they are lacking a suitable partner. I understand. This world does not reward women who can do for themselves. You will look out into the world and people will tell you that you are not dependent enough. You will hear that you need to be more helpless in order to find a guy. I offer this to you. The problem is not that you are too strong. The problem is that the men today are too weak. Too many men are not taking their rightful place as Men. Men are offering up excuses as to why they cannot perform and why their "balls" are missing. I also have to say that there are strong men out there that are not being recognized. I have to say to you, "what kinds of women are you chasing?" The only advice that I can offer to you is, "It's your choice." How much are you willing to compromise in order to have a partner?

I know that strong does not keep you warm at night. Strong does not help you carry the groceries inside. Strong does not call you on the phone, or send you a text, or an email throughout the day. You cannot make love to strong in the middle of the night. You cannot watch a movie and talk about it with Strength. So, what will you sacrifice in order to have those things? Respect.

Tell me how it feels to lay down with a man you don't respect and who doesn't respect you. Tell me what it feels like to have a man carry groceries that you paid for. Tell me what it feels like to encourage a man to pursue his dreams and watch him sit down on himself because of fear. Tell me what it feels like to listen to a man offer every excuse in the book about why he cannot do something. I want to know your thoughts when he compares you to women who are weaker than you. How did it feel when he glorified women who like to play the victim and sit down on themselves, so he can feel more like a man? "She cried, so that means that she is really hurt. You never cry. You'll be okay. I never have to worry about you." Where was your reward, when you continued in spite of? Where was your plaque when you fought to get what was rightfully yours? Where was your recognition for not falling apart when things got tough?

The problem is nowadays, men would rather be the king of mud, than be the king of brick, just as long as they can call themselves king. Strength, determination, perseverance, ability, vision, and independent thinking are often no longer valued qualities in your community. Since the men often do not posses those qualities, it is frowned upon for you to hold them. So, men and women what is your response? Can we turn time around to when women were strong and men were even stronger?

If both people in a relationship showed strength, determination, forward thinking, and faith, there would be no stopping their force. But when one partner is weak and the other is strong, you can only move as far as the weakest one. **When both partners are weak, there is no forward movement.**

I would like to submit to you today, men and women, the following: There should be no value in weakness and fear. Every member should be strong. The time for talking and not walking is over. The time for dreaming and not doing is over. The time for blame and excuses is over. If you have the knowledge to do something and haven't done

70

it, then you are contributing to weakness. Everyone has the capacity to be great, but it's only those who believe in their greatness who actually accomplish great things. Fear is the major hindrance that separates people from greatness. Your relationship should be great. Your relationship should be an example of the success that is in you. Two people are a powerful force. Why do relationships demonstrate 1.5 or 1.0 or 0.5?

It is time for both men and women to be great. It is time for both partners to contribute 1000%. There is no time for anyone to sit down on their relationship. Everyone has a duty and a function and a responsibility to give all that they can to the other person. If your relationship is lacking, then you are the one who is slacking!

What Dis-Ease Plagues Men?

Men, no more excuses for anything. **You are a MAN**. There is nothing that you cannot accomplish. You are the head of the family. You set the tone of the relationship. It is your responsibility to move forward. It is your responsibility to have the vision for the relationship. The reason that some of you don't know how to find the vision is because you have not found the Source for sight. God is your source (whichever deity you serve) whether you recognize it or not. Stop looking around at other lost men to provide you answers and instruction on how to be a man. Find men who are changing the world. Find men who are doing something positive. Find men who are leaders of themselves and their families. Look for men who show and receive respect, not just from other men, but their families and women too. I mean mature women, not "little girls".

The most important thing for you to do is to find value and worth within yourself. Why be the king of a mud hut, when you can be the king of a brick palace? As soon as you decide the kind of man you want to be, you will be able to pick a woman that represents, respects, and encourages your worth. Many of you have picked weak, negative women with no vision that have encouraged you to go nowhere, that show you no respect, and that undervalue everything you do. After a while of residing and becoming one with these women, your value in your own eyes will decrease. Along with the removal of your worth and your value, will be the removal of your "balls". That is how we have ended up with so many weak and impotent men in our communities. Men, make a choice today. **Brains should be the first thing you value in a woman instead of booty.** Again, do you want to be the king of a mud hut or king of a brick palace? The choice is yours.

Side note: A brick palace not only "has your back", but your front and your sides too. (For those who don't understand, it means that this person will support, defend, protect, look ahead for, and cheer you on in everything you do, no matter what circumstances arise.) With a "brick palace", you will be well fortified and able to withstand any attack. All of your pleasures will be within its gates, and your demonstration to the outside world will be one of success. It is what allows you to go forward into the world to achieve, because you know that your home is stable.

Men, if you are trying to make the transition from a mud hut to a brick palace, then you are going to have to change your strategy. A leader is more than just calling yourself one by name. A leader has confidence in himself and in his abilities. He is not intimidated or threatened by another strong presence. You have to know in your heart of hearts that you belong at the top, and you have to believe that you are supposed to be in that position. If you are able to find yourself a ruler over a brick palace, then the concurrence is there. Meaning, if a strong woman allows you to be the "head" of her (the king, the ruling force, the benefactor, the one she looks to) then she already believes that you are capable of being in that position. This means that she recognizes that you are a leader. Now that this issue is settled, you should be able to move on with progress.

Once it has been established that you are the leader, the most important factor now is your team. The biggest demonstration of your effectiveness and success is shown in the progress and motivation of your team. The first and most important step is to recognize what kind of player you have. Again, since you have moved from the mud hut, you are going to have to alter your strategy.

Side note: If you are really controlling then a mud hut may be good for you. That way, you can control every step.

In the past, you would have to tell a mud hut what the play was and then give detailed, step by step instructions on how to carry it out. For example, you say that you want Thanksgiving Dinner. Then you have to tell her what to buy, where to get it, how to prepare it, and why it is important. Then if one of the things on your list is not there, she will call you fifteen times to ask questions, or in the alternative, just give up all together. This translates to the business of the relationship as well. For example, a pipe bursts in the house, and you are at work. She calls you at work to tell you that a pipe burst, and she doesn't know what to do. She wants you to take care of it and work your job too. Meanwhile, your house is filling up with water. So, you tell her to call the plumber and get the number out of the phone book. She calls the plumber, but she doesn't understand what he's saying. So, she calls you again at work to tell you that you need to call the plumber and talk to him and figure everything out. So, that's what you do. When you get home, she is mad and frustrated with you because you weren't there to take care of everything and she is so stressed out.

This is not the case with a brick palace. You tell the brick palace what you need done and move on to another task. Let's use the example of the Thanksgiving Dinner again. If she is familiar with Thanksgiving Dinner, then she will make all of the necessary preparations. She will call you one time towards the end to verify what has been done and to see if you have any last minute suggestions. In the alternative, if she has not encountered a Thanksgiving Dinner, then she will research what is required and continue the task of making it happen. And when you get home from work, the conversation goes like this: "One of the pipes burst today and the house started flooding. I called the plumber and he came over, fixed the leak, and dried the floor. The bill is over on the table." Now some of you can't have that conversation, because you are not in the position to have a palace yet.

Since your teams have different make-ups, your strategy for motivation and understanding the plights of the players are different. If you are giving advice about a situation to your brick palace, provide your input and allow her to vent. Once she has vented her frustration, she will ponder your advice and probably ask for suggestions in bettering her situation.

Side note: This is why it is important for you as a leader to always seek wisdom, so that you will have a successful response. Pray for it if you don't possess it.

What a lot of men do in this circumstance is to become frustrated and think that their insight is not being respected. They take the woman venting to mean that she doesn't respect his authority, and then they say something negative against her character (normally something about her rebellion against authority or her doing things on her own so much that she doesn't recognize help or a blessing when she receives it) in order to tear her down, to weaken her. This attempt to weaken her is really in response to your lack of feeling strong and your intimidation. You feel as though she is challenging your authority. Men, this is where you should already be convinced that you are a leader. **The only challenge to your authority has been made by you.** If you listen closely to her complaint, it is not about YOU, but about weakness in other people. In the earlier example, the mud hut was complaining about her own weakness.

Further, if you weaken your strongest player, then that would be disastrous for you. Why tear down the walls of your palace? That will make your defenses weaker and make you more susceptible to attacks. Once you have eliminated your protection, then your dynasty will begin to crumble. The new strategy is to fortify and strengthen your palace-shore up any holes. Motivate her and give her the keys to be more successful in her situation. If you do, she will know how to handle it from that moment on. Let's recap 1) know that you are the leader in your heart of hearts, 2) know that your team believes you are the leader, 3) don't be intimidated by strong players, 4) recognize the qualities of your players and adapt your strategy based on their characteristics, and finally 5) cultivate and motivate your team to be the most successful players out there.

Women: Your Cause Should Be Effect

Women, no more dependency is allowed. You have a responsibility to yourself and to your family to be intelligent. It is no longer acceptable to hide your mental acuity. The best way to support a man is to be able to carry your own weight. If a man is going to be strong, you have to understand situations. As women, we should be able to think logically. Reacting with our emotions is not always the best response to situations. We have to be able to pick up the tasks that our men cannot cover. **No one person can do everything.** It is a TEAM effort.

Women have vision too. Your vision of the pathway to success should coincide with the man's vision. If you are thinking "left" and the man is thinking "right", how much time are the both of you wasting by arguing over directions? Get with a man whose vision and style align with yours. In that way, when the man calls out "right", you can say "good idea" and keep it moving. For example, there may be a higher position at your man's job, which he desires. His approach to success may be to work his way up into the spot. Your idea for success may be for him to storm in and demand the position. The ultimate goal is to attain the higher status, what you are arguing over is approach.

What Kind of King Do You Want?

So many relationships are stagnant because the man and the woman are fighting over which way to go. There is no movement in a consistent argument. While you are standing there proving your point, time and opportunity are passing you by. **The true argument that you are having is over perception and expectation.** If you desire that he storms in and takes the position, this speaks a lot about your idea of a "Man". The examples of men that have been provided to you either by your family or by environment, dictate that this is the behavior that men should display. His idea of working his way into a position may be how he has seen it done by men in his experience. Neither of you are wrong, you just approach situations differently. Your perception of a man's behavior and your expectation of how a man performs are different from his. This kind of conflict in perception and expectation is what causes the respect to be lost in the relationship. You have to identify what kind of king that you want. What kind of leadership style do you require? What kind of leadership style do you respect? I promise you that there is someone out there that thinks just like you. Also, you are not always right. Sometimes, the man has the vision and if you would trust him, you would get to where you want to be. **Allow your man to be a man.** There may be aspects of the situation that you don't know about. He may not be able to storm in because he may have to win people to his side in order to be successful and effective.

Everyone makes mistakes and he will too and so will you. Why would you destroy his desire to move forward? If he sits down, so does your entire relationship. You want your man out there making progress. Progress only comes by forward movement. The only way that you will make

76

progress together is if you support him. Encourage him in his endeavors, and he will bring you with him. He will share his plans with you. He will tell you what he's thinking. Then you will have a chance to offer your input, and he will consider it. The only way you can offer valuable input is if you are intelligent. You have to be able to think with logic and reasoning. You have to be able to look at a situation and ponder most of the sides. You have eyes and a vision too. You should be able to bring up things that he hasn't thought of, but in a positive way. So, women, be strong within yourself, so that your man can be strong for both of you.

Strong women I offer this chapter to you as hope that you will be able to find a man that wants to take his rightful place in the world. I hope that men desire to be stronger, instead of desiring that you become weaker.

"I can't force you and tell you where you belong. You have to already know your place." –Ocean Shaw

Chapter Ten

CONCLUSION

"The most perfect kind of love is expressed not physically but intellectually."   **-Plato** *Symposium*

YOU HAVE THE KEY TO YOUR LIFE'S SUCCESS- the answer is in knowing where to find it. Every day we are presented with images of success and failure. We see the greatest of people rise high and fall low. We witness their joys and their excitement, along with their hurt and their pain. In every moment, we watch this remarkably talented person form and shape their life based on their decisions and this person is you.

Everything in your life stops and starts with you. This does not mean that you control what happens to you, but your choices, based on given circumstances, are what shape the direction of your life. Improved and favorable decisions, which lead to more success, can come by a better recognition of your "self". So, if you search within to discover who you are, then you can begin the transition to the life you've always wanted because you **are** the key to your life's success.

Just as the quote above suggests, the physical chemistry involved in finding a partner seems to happen automatically, but the success of our relationships depend on our intellect-our thoughts, perceptions, and expectations. Before we can think of entering into a relationship with anyone, we should have a firm understanding of "self", so that we don't sabotage the bond needed for a lasting connection. The best way to develop a firm understanding of self is to look inward and discover our own distinctiveness.

When we look inside of ourselves and discover the thoughts and perceptions that control our actions, we are able to establish our own identity and shed those portions of ourselves that are negative or defeating. Sometimes this involves acknowledging the presence of a negative aspect of our personality or dealing with past disappointments and experiences that have caused us pain. During the process of discovering self and establishing identity, we start to become a more whole person. We no longer look to others to define us and tell us who we are and what we are not. We have confidence in our abilities and our appearance, and we are able to make better decisions for our lives and our future. Favorable decisions and acknowledgment of our core being allow us to align with our needs, resulting in an overall happier person.

The ability to align ourselves with our needs means that we are being true to ourselves. When we act in accordance with our needs, we lessen the feeling of lack and depravity in our lives. It is important to focus on our needs, because needs are a strong driving force that motivates us into action. Some of the "bad" decisions we have made in life, started with a perceived need that was not being met. Some of the people that we allowed to be the closest to us were the ones to hurt us the most. We brought them close because we thought that they filled a gaping hole in our lives. We expected them to heal and save us from the things that threaten to unravel us and tear us down. The responsibility to heal our pain is a huge burden to place on a person, and almost everyone fails at this mission, because they need healing too. Then after we've been hurt by this "savior", we move from person to person looking for the next "healer". In the end, all we are left with is a bigger and bigger hole-creating more gaping space.

The only person who can fill this hole is you. The only person who can jump start the process to healing is you. You are the only person who can change your situation. The answer-the key is inside of you. Healing comes by visiting the source of the issue and working your way up from there. The source of the issue always starts with you. It can be true that the hurt or the pain or the action causing both was performed against you, but if you wait for the person who hurt you to apologize, healing may never come. There are people who die every day who have never apologized to the ones they've hurt, and there are people who die who have never heard the words, "I'm sorry". Things are going to happen that are out of your control-but in every negative situation, there are things you CAN control-your reaction, your thoughts, and how you allow the situation affect you. These three things are in your control. You have a choice of whether you allow someone's actions to create baggage in your life or not. Remember, what you accept and what you choose to carry is carried only by you. The person who has hurt you will not carry this baggage, this hurt, this pain, or this disappointment. Only you will bear the weight of this burden, and only you will carry this weight year after year and from person to person.

Decide to release the baggage of pain and hurt from your grip, and instead pick up peace, joy, understanding and happiness. Instead of feeling and playing the victim, feel and act like the victor. You are now stronger and more refined because of negative situations. If your adversity did not kill you, then everything was a lesson in order to expose those parts of you that need changing or that need attention. The next step is to use wisdom to evaluate all sides of the situation. We need wisdom in order to discover the inherent problems in our circumstance, make better choices in our future, and to heal the pain of the lesson. When we evaluate a situation using wisdom, we are able to determine why the situation had to end and why we cannot continue to exist under those circumstances. This evaluation is what eliminates the accumulation of baggage and allows us to use better judgment when we move on with our lives.

Once our thoughts and perceptions are healed then our communication will begin to change. We won't be so ready to argue and express our negative feelings to others. A lot of what we say starts with our thoughts. If we are thinking of pain and hurt, then our communication reveals those thoughts. If we are insecure or lacking in trust, what we say to others and how we interpret their actions will make our speech accusatory. When we are dissatisfied with our situation, then our words turn into complaints. In order to be a person who speaks with encouragement and a person who is able to inspire others, you have to first have those feelings and thoughts within you. How can you thinking negative, lead to anything positive? When this is the case, even when we try to mask our true feelings, our words end up having a condescending or mocking tone. If you change your thoughts, then you can change your speech, which will strengthen your "self" and your relationships.

We are not separate from our words. We are accountable for everything that we say. Our words have life, and if we continually speak "death and destruction" over our relationships, then that is what we will end up with. If we consistently say harmful and damaging things to people, then those words will take root in the minds of the person who heard them. Words, especially words that are negative remain in the hearer's thoughts, playing over and over like a recording. Eventually, the hearer's perception and feelings for you (the person who spoke negatively) will take on the form of your message. Meaning, the exact feeling that you were looking to create in that person by your harmful words, will be created, but **the feeling will be towards you**. Do you want out of your relationship? Do you want your connection (spark, fire, intimacy) eliminated? If you do, then continue speaking destructively. However, if you are looking to have a healthy relationship, provide encouragement, compliments, kind words of rebuke and inspiration. Use honey not vinegar. There is no winning in tearing a person down, instead everyone loses.

A lot of arguments and disagreements in relationships are spawned from a person's feeling of lack and insufficiency. So, again it is important to identify your core needs and not settle for superficial desires. It is nice to be able to spend time with someone, but the connection should be deeper than being able to watch television together. There is a lot more to a person than their physical appearance or their attempt to put their best foot forward. All physicality is fleeting. The only thing that we are left with in our relationships is the connection with the real inner person. The inner person is the person who actually enters the relationship, both your inner person and your partner's.

Even in the act of sex, we ultimately are dealing with the inner man. The thoughts of a person as he or she approaches the bed have an effect on the actions of the person while in the throws of sex. Either way, our thoughts, perceptions, and expectations are brought into the bedroom with us, and are in motion before we even touch the other person. So, if you want to have a fulfilling sex life, then discover the mind-frame of your partner and see if it lines up with your own outlook of sex.

Sex is also one of the areas where people recognize and are willing to acknowledge compromise, but many of us have compromised long before we entered the bedroom. The purpose of this book is to remind you that compromising your needs may lead to a lifetime of unhappiness and want. In order to make sure that we are not compromising our "selves"-which is really our inner man-our soul, then we have to be familiar with what our inner man needs. Once we are familiar with our needs, we have to be true or faithful to those needs and requirements, if we are going to be "successful" and happy.

When there is pain or frustration in our lives, it is because of our decisions-what we decided to forgo or ignore.

These decisions, causing pain, seem to build and spiral to a point where we have no idea of who we are or how we got there (the place of pain and frustration). Oftentimes, once we begin to realize that we are in a negative place, instead of evaluating the situation, we begin to adopt the negativity as our identity. Let us stop this self-fulfilling spiral of negative actions becoming negative thoughts resulting in more negative actions. Be honest and be true to yourself (act in accordance with your needs). There is nothing wrong with you except you are trying to be someone you are not. You are not the messed up person that you may think you are. There is a beautiful person inside who deserves to be happy and loved, just like everyone else. You just have to find this remarkable person and get more acquainted them. You have to show your inner person more attention and allow them to make decisions with you. Don't starve your "self". After you introduce yourself, love your "self" and respect your "self". Your inner person is the one who suffers when you make questionable decisions.

As for relationships, there is someone out there that can be satisfied with you just the way you are, but you have to be patient and honest about what you need. Most of us don't want to wait for the BEST option, and instead settle for someone good or less than that, because we think some imaginary clock is running out. Why put that kind of pressure on yourself? You have the rest of your life to spend with that person, why choose poorly? You'll just end up divorced five years later or miserable fifty years later. If some of us were willing to be honest, we would admit that we are attached to a person that is not the best fit for us. The reason that you seem to not be getting along is because you have not found a partner that mirrors you. Use this book to hold a mirror up to yourself to establish your own identity and to reconnect with your inner man inside, so you will be able to recognize your best fit when you meet them. It will be so much more worth it in the long run. You have the key to your success, but it is up to you to use it. You can turn your life around and make the rest of your years more fulfilling or you can continue the spiral of hurt and negativity. I know that it will be hard to deal with your past, but it will be the best way to secure a more positive and healthy future. Pain is a part of growth and without growth, we will not be mature or strong. I hope that from this moment forth all of your needs will be met and that you are able to find your BEST partner for a wonderful long-lasting relationship.

-Ocean

*Go to www.oceanshaw.com for additional comments.

ACKNOWLEDGMENTS

I want to express my sincere thanks to all of the following people:

The ILL Genius   Thanks for the support and words of encouragement.   **www.psourcemusic.com**

Ashland Johnson, one of the most accommodating and most honest editors around. Thank you for your time and diligence.

Ricko Swink and Sharon Bazil-Thank you for building a very professional website for me. You have really captured my personality and given life to my ideas.
www.rickoworldwide.com

Evan Kaine, Esq.-Thank you for the contract review and business advice.   **www.kainelaw.com**

Infinity Publishing, Inc.-Thank you for putting my dream into print.   **www.infinitypublishing.com**

Daniel Barnett-Marketing & Promotions
www.dbpevents.com

Jerbrina Johnson, Esq.-Thank you for the wonderful foreword.

Lamont Bell

Atiba Long

Shari Singleton

NATIONAL HOTLINES

Alcohol and Drug Helpline-for adolescents and adults

    1-800-821-4357

Child Abuse National Hotline

    1-800-252-2873

Domestic Violence Resource Hotline

    1-800-799-7233 or 1-800-787-3224

National Mental Health Association

    1-800-969-6642

Suicide National Hotlines

    1-800-SUICIDE   1-800-784-2433

    1-800-273-TALK   1-800-273-8255

US Department of Health and Human Services' Substance Abuse and Mental Health Services Administration (SAMHSA) may have additional information for help in your area.

www.healthyplace.com

www.ulifeline.org

Consult the appropriate professionals within your state or city.

Disclaimer: Be aware that these phone numbers offered as help or sources for help may have changed or disappeared between the time this book was written and when this book is read.

CPSIA information can be obtained at www.ICGtesting.com
Printed in the USA
LVOW070532250313

325662LV00007B/65/P